Piso Christ

(A Book of the New Classical Scholarship)

Arrius Calpurnius Piso
aka Flavius Josephus
The Roman Inventor of The Biblical Jesus,
The New Testament Story, and Christianity

Roman Piso
In Collaboration with
Jay Gallus

(The information in this book has never before been published is such specific detail)

Order this book online at www.trafford.com
or email orders@trafford.com

Most Trafford titles are also available at major online book retailers.

Printed in Victoria, BC, Canada.

ISBN: 978-1-4269-2996-0 (sc)
ISBN: 978-1-4269-3044-7 (hc)

Library of Congress Control Number: 2010904711

*Our mission is to efficiently provide the world's finest, most comprehensive book publishing
service, enabling every author to experience success. To find out how to publish your book, your
way, and have it available worldwide, visit us online at www.trafford.com*

Trafford rev. 07/06/2010

Trafford
PUBLISHING   www.trafford.com

North America & international
toll-free: 1 888 232 4444 (USA & Canada)
phone: 250 383 6864 ♦ fax: 812 355 4082

Table of Contents

INTRODUCTION TO 'PISO CHRIST!'

This work represents a tremendous amount of research, done during a period of many years. It consists primarily of a collection of essays and articles relating to the subject of the actual authorship of the New Testament, and the invention of Jesus and Christianity; as well as the history of that time.

PISO CHRIST! is just one of several books that we have written about this particular subject. The difference of the level of scholarship represented by the various books is intentional. The only other 'book' that has been available, specifically written about the Roman family named Piso, as the writers of the New Testament, is the booklet *"The True Authorship of The New Testament"* by Abelard Reuchlin. It is a very scholarly work that may have been too academic and not explanatory enough for general understanding.

Therefore, the thought here was, there should be material available to act as a sort of 'bridge' to the more scholarly material on which we have been working. Other books are also necessary to explain this research to persons who would prefer and understand our findings on a more scholarly level. Thus, the need for books explaining this subject in detail on various levels of scholarship.

This book is prepared for the general public who will and need to learn the truth about the subject herein presented, and should thereby establish a foundation of people who have learned and understand this important information. This is to allow, no matter what happens, that the information itself could not be 'lost', destroyed or taken away from the public. It would be there, no matter what happens. That was the primary consideration for taking this to the people firstly.

After many people have read and understand this information, the case could be presented to academia. And, therefore, perhaps the need for the more scholarly books. When this information gets into the world of academia, is presented and explained on that level, this will cause a change in academia itself, and the way that people think worldwide. In short, it will change by necessity, as what will be realized is, that history itself did not, and could not have happened in the way in which it has been taught, accepted and believed. This, in turn, will allow for history to be much more available and visible, more understandable, and better known to the general public. Because, in effect, academia as the authority in scholarship will release all of this information to the public, making it finally known to everyone. Then will come the effect of changing the focus of academia so that it will change its aims and resources in this area, allowing for many more books that will be written about this subject. Eventually knowledge and the truth about this subject, rather than fantasy, mysticism and tall tales as now, will bring full freedom of mind to all, and will then be a part of our natural everyday lives that has been hidden from the public for too many centuries.

Here are titles of other books in which we present more on this subject matter. *"The Synthesis of Christianity," "The Origin of Christianity - A New Millennium Of Scholarship," "Pliny: Words and Phrases."* In our research for the truth about the making of the Christian religion, through the critical examination of the New Testament texts, we have found examples of the same methods used by magicians; namely, the art of 'redirection'.

At times during a conversation one may want to make a specific point on a subject, but the other person in the conversation may not want to respond to the point being made, and may try to *change the subject* or pretend not to be interested. That is one form of redirection.

In a magic trick, the magician is generally in control of the attention of the audience by causing them to focus upon one thing, while doing another where they are NOT looking. That is 'redirection'. Sometimes a magician will apply this or something similar, where the eye must follow an object in order to keep track of it. Another trick using redirection is, when a person seems to remove a coin out of or from behind someone's ear.

In literature, redirection can be used as a form of persuasion, or more directly, as a basis for propaganda. An example of the use of redirection can be a specifically worded question that guides listeners or readers to think in one certain way, instead of the way they would mostly likely think and answer. A question that is deliberately 'formulated' (as opposed to an original, honestly worded question) is one that can be broken down to reveal ulterior motives needed to obtain the answer desired by the person asking the question. Such a question is sometimes referred to as a "loaded question".

A couple of such questions could be something similar to: "WHO created us?" "WHO created the planets?" How can we know these questions are not honest, and that they were 'formulated'? Because, such questions are actually rhetoric. The word 'who' is intended to lead persons to a preconceived conclusion. The only 'who' that comes quickly to the uninformed or untrained mind in such a question, without thinking, is 'God'. So, there is the element of presupposition, causing the listener to agree as the speaker desires. The question guided the listener's attention to 'creationism' by use of the word 'created'. Therefore, the answer is built into such a question; a loaded question. By using such questions, the person asking the question can block out other more thoughtful answers, and is redirecting thought and conversation. Questions such as this were invented by priests and others who had a vested interest in causing the minds of the masses to think in certain ways; to accept without thinking, nor questioning what they have been taught and told to believe.

What this really means is, that the subject of religion, the invention and building of Christianity and even ancient history itself, is much more complicated than the vast majority of scholars have considered up to this point in time. That is because all of these areas involved royals (persons who presented themselves to the masses as being royalty and above others), were in control of everything for thousands of years, and they were extremely well educated and intelligent.

The way in which the Christian, and other ancient texts have been observed by scholars until now, is from the point of view that they were written primarily by common people who were uneducated for the most part; this is so particularly true in the case of the Christian texts. We have been working to prove that this is not true, and those who created Christianity, were in fact much more intelligent than most people today can begin to imagine. As royals, they had access to a vast and most exceptional library of knowledge and information on anything known to man at the time.

Information about those who put this work into the form of this book:

In many books, today you will find a section, which is usually titled something like "About The Author." This is an area where there is some information given about the author of the work. But, this particular subject is one which does not lend that kind of openness about the persons who composed this work. The reason being is, that there are bound to be some people who will misuse this information and may use it as a means to attack the writers.

True scholars realize that it is the information itself, which is of importance, and this is because if it is true, it will still be true no matter WHO presents it. Some people tend to not consider the possible need of anonymity. For instance, consider a person who has some very important information that all people need to know. We are talking about information that may play a large part in changing the way people conduct themselves worldwide, but there are other people, groups, and organizations which do not want that information to become known to the general public. And the person(s) who composed the information may be the only person(s) who know enough about the subject to present it in detailed written form, or perhaps is (are) among the very, very few who can and are willing to inform both academia and the general public. There will no doubt be people who will try to harm, if not try to kill them in order to silence their presentation of truth. Such persons must remain anonymous, at least at the beginning of presenting such important work of truth that has been kept from the general public for hundreds and in some cases perhaps for thousands of years.

I, Roman Piso, feel that I am put into this situation and that I must consider the value of my life to humanity, above possible fame and a life of celebrity. I do not think that I would live long enough to enjoy any celebrity if everyone knew my full identity now. The only way that I think to be able to make all of this known is to have several books published and have a majority of people educated on this subject - as that would greatly reduce the possibility of anyone trying to harm me personally, and at which point it would make very little difference.

But, indeed I did promise certain persons to say a bit here about myself. I have written books and articles for many years as 'Roman Piso'. I am a descendant of the Piso family. This is true, but not as amazing as many people may currently think. Discovery of this information came about while researching ancient history and my own family tree. I have cousins in Romania who have traced the modern Piso family in Romania back to thirteenth century Italy. But there are family members who are descendants of the Roman Piso family that no longer use the Piso name; because though they are still descendants, they used other names in order to create new branches of the family. If I say too much about myself now, I may not live long enough to participate in writing the other books that truly need to be written. In addition, I am sure that if you think about this you will understand my point.

Where I, Jay Gallus am concerned, being perhaps more out-spoken than Roman Piso, there are individuals and organizations that are known to me which do not want the information contained in this book to be placed into the hands of the general public. The world needs to know the information between the pages of this book and other books on which we are working. However, beyond anonymity, we remind people of just what is the purpose for presenting this written work. It is to make this information, this valuable truth about a certain time in history, available to the general public, so that they may do their own research on the subject if they so choose. Research of this subject does not mean asking your preacher or priest, because he or she will give to you a long winded story that will not answer your question. The true meaning of the New Testament story was never intended to be understood by its believers, because if they could have learned the truth about Christianity when they were being indoctrinated into believing what they were taught, they would not have become a believer or surely would not have remained as a believer.

By placing this information in the hands of the general public, will allow that a large number of people will learn of it, so that it will spark an interest in many of them to go on to learn more about this so as to become more informed on this subject. When this occurs, a foundation will be established from which more study of this subject in academia will result. It is as a question raised, which will need to be answered.

Regarding the writing of books about this subject for academia, as has already been said, true scholars realize that it is true information which is important - not WHO has supplied it. Therefore, academia will be able to examine the information and make reasonable assessments upon learning about it. None of which requires knowing anything personally about either one of the composers. Therefore, there isn't any valid reason for giving any more personal information about ourselves for the present time.

In addition, Abelard Reuchlin had done some radio interviews in the 1980's. During that time, he was in contact with Sir Ronald Syme. Syme was a researcher on our level, but he did not write openly about what we now know. He had much to lose had he done so, as he was very highly regarded by the scholars of classical history of that time. Abelard Reuchlin had considered Syme to be 'Inner-Circle' (meaning that he was aware of the fact that the history of the time in which Christianity was invented and built was controlled by the Roman royals and this included the Piso family).

He wrote several articles for the JRS (Journal of Roman Studies). The real work supporting the findings of the N.C.S. (New Classical Scholarship) comes from scholars who did not realize the true meaning of what they had contributed to academia. Their work also contributed to others who have held very high positions in traditional scholarship, and knew more than they could talk about many years ago. Moreover, many references, many times have come from many other researchers. So when viewed carefully, what has been done here is, to bring together the work of others and our own research which has gone even further and, put it together in a way that explains its true meaning.

This is about finding the truth by following all leads and questionable written history, a new view, a new perspective, that will be seen to be the truth, as it explains ancient history; whereas before, many questions were left unanswered. Besides the people mentioned above, there are those who we term 'Transitional Classical Scholars' (T.C.S.), and are among those who do not know about the Piso Project or the New Classical Scholarship, but whose work either has come to the same conclusions or supports the findings of the N.C.S. These are important scholars, such as Jacob Neusner, and Prof. Randel Helms. Those who are of the T.C.S. are the scholars who are most likely to be receptive to our information and to the N.C.S.

Regarding the book titled *'Caesar's Messiah'* by Joseph Atwill, scholars are saying that, "if Atwill is correct, this spells the end of Christianity". Atwill argues that "the reason scholars have not figured out the truth about Christianity, is because they have been viewing the New Testament as a religious document, when in fact, it is actually satire!" That is actually correct, as the story does not represent what believers of Christianity have been taught to believe, think and blindly accept, but it was written as a parody and is satire representing an entirely different event.

On page 26 of his book; Atwill says ".... the NT was also designed to be understood in another way, that is as a satire of Titus Flavius' military campaign through Judea. The proof of this is simply that Jesus and Titus shared parallel experiences at the same locations, at the same time, and in the same sequence. Parallels that were, both too exact and too complex to have occurred by chance. This fact has to have been intentionally disregarded for nearly two thousand years, which represents a blind spot in scholarship as large as the length of time is long that this has not been found and the truth not presented." Yes, Atwill has made a powerful case for the Roman invention of Christianity. However, Titus was not in Judea leading the Roman military alone.

FOREWORD TO 'PISO CHRIST!'

There was a time when we may have thought that people who studied and taught history actually knew what they were talking about and understood the nature of history. However, we have learned that the truth is, they were really working from a foundation of assumptions (for more see the BACKGROUND section). While studying "The True Authorship of the New Testament" and the beginnings of the Christian religion, answers to what seemed to be very important questions were thought to be necessary, but after realizing the obvious, these questions were not needed. This is what the general public needs to know, that a virtual hand-full of people were the original creators of not only the Christian religion, but they were also the authors of the New Testament and the history of that time. Only they and others who helped in certain ways could have had the awesome power to have achieved this goal. How could this have happened? How could those few persons have that much power, and why were they able to succeed? They were acting more as 'front-men' for the majority of royals at the time. This was done on behalf of the majority of royals and with their backing. Those royals all had the same stake in what they could gain from making the religion called Christianity.

Then, the questions become; "did this begin with these people at that time?" "Did the royals have complete control over all that was written for public consumption beginning with these people or did it pre-exist? The answer that was found is, that it HAD to pre-exist, as that is what royals had always done. All royals were bound, and connected, and many were related to each other in ways that most people have never even considered. They all had in common, their own shared legitimacy (ability/right) to rule over the masses. This, in turn, brings us to the point of understanding that, at least on occasions, they worked with each other to help preserve that institution which their own ancestors had created – allowing them the right to rule as royals.

xvi | *Piso Christ*

As we learned more and more, the reality becomes known that ancient royals created various concepts and put those out to the public in the form of books and other written works, or through speeches, to have those concepts taught to and believed by the uninformed masses over which they ruled. They had invented the concept of gods so that there would be a 'higher power' which they could claim had given them the right to rule over others. Their invented "higher power" would be used to legitimize their rule over the common people. The term brain-washing may not have been known at that time in history, but that is exactly what the royals and ruling-class were doing.

The concept of gods did (1) provided the ordaination, and what the masses thought was the legitimate right given to the royals by a god to rule over them. After the royals presented gods as the 'higher power' who, they claimed, confirmed them to be the choice above any others to be the rulers, the masses were then taught to be afraid of the gods. (2) the royals used the god-concept to put fear into the people so that they would not dare challenge the royals. The result was that the people would not even think of overthrowing the so-called ordained (god chosen representatives) for fear of (as they were taught) the wrath of the gods. That, is the real reason why and how the concept of gods was developed. It is how the royals were able to do what they desired. That is the reason also for religions and royals to become so closely connected and supportive, each of the other. It was well thought out and planned; both to be hidden and then revealed. It did not come about because of the god concept represented in the Bible, which is not real nor natural. Even Adam, mentioned in the Old Testament, was royalty, and obviously used the god-concept over his people, and that god-concept is still used over millions of people today, and it is not natural, and millions are being fooled into accepting the concept of a god, then they live in fear of a totally unnatural belief.

Persons who were thinking of ways to keep themselves in power over the majority of people, used the concept of god or gods in conjunction with others to achieve their control over the uninformed masses. They were the persons who developed the god-concept. They knew that knowledge was power and, therefore, did whatever they could to keep the masses ignorant and superstitious. Unfortunately, they did a very good job of this and all of the things that they had put into place so long ago are still a large part of the lives of many people to this day. (3) as a part of the creation of gods, they also had to develop religion around those gods so that they would reap the benefits in the form of huge amounts of various wealth.

Realizing the fact that no one was writing other than royals, limits the possible authors of any given work at any given time, so that it becomes a matter of finding which royals were living in particular areas at a specific time in order to learn who were the possible authors. Knowing this, we began the process of elimination so that we could isolate the possible candidates and from those, further deduce (given a number of relevant facts), the most probable authors and, from there find the actual authors.

So, there is a process to go through in order that determinations as to authorship can be finally and reliably revealed and confirmed by the indicating comments and inferences made by the authors themselves. Profiles are also a part of this process, a very necessary part and, the reason is that the authors hid information on various 'levels'. Some of these are very well hidden or camouflaged and require a very advanced knowledge of the people, places, and events of the time in addition to a deep knowledge of the works of all of the authors of that time. And, of course, a very good working knowledge of the ancient languages that were being used. As you can now understand, this was a long process of learning about one thing, and that one thing led to discovery of another thing that made that prior thing possible. It is like the adage, "one thing leads to another".

SIR RONALD SYME, AND ABELARD REUCHLIN

Abelard Reuchlin had tried to educate several scholars to the fact that Sir Ronald Syme was privy to the fact that the Roman Piso family invented the Jesus story and the Christian religion and, that they were successful because they were also in control of all that was being written for public consumption at the time - biblical or not. Reuchlin had tried to explain to scholars the reason that Syme was able to write in such detail in all of the various areas of Roman history that he wrote about, because he was looking at it with the great advantage of 'seeing' it from the inside looking out at those who did not understand what he knew. Only by being 'Inner-Circle' could he draw the conclusions and raise the kind of questions that he did. As a matter of fact, Syme's work is what had made it possible for other 'Inner-Circle' members to make more progress in their own research. Abelard Reuchlin and other I.C. members had been reading Syme's work for many years, from which much information was gathered. (More mention of Syme's particular works is in the Bibliography of this book). The death of Sir Ronald Syme, even though he was quite elderly, came as a great shock to many people who had been following his work. He was born in 1903 and died in September of 1989. A British historian by profession, he studied and taught at Oxford University. He was a patriotic Brit, serving the British government both in Belgrade and in Ankara during WWII. Syme had been a Fellow at Trinity College, Oxford from 1929 to 1949. He was a professor of Classical Philology and taught at the University of Istanbul from 1942 to 1945, and Camden professor of ancient texts and, Fellow at Brasenose College, Oxford from 1949 to 1970, as well as a Fellow of Wolfson College, Oxford from 1970 up to 1989.

Sir Ronald Syme was an eminent scholar of classical Rome and, very well respected by his peers. However, he was also wise enough to realize the fact that had he tried to publicly present his findings as we are doing now, he would have suffered the same fate as Bruno Bauer - he would have lost all of the credibility that he had gained in the world of academia. This is because it is a vastly huge task to compile and publish all of this information into a comprehensive form which people can readily understand. It requires many things which most people, even scholars, are not used to - including learning many completely new and different concepts while examining everything with a very objective and agile mind. This subject matter is not 'easy', and must be researched in an open-minded manner. Syme simply realized the truth of the situation and went quietly about his work, knowing that his research would help future generations after they realize the underlying truth about ancient history.

Syme wrote the well-known *'Roman Revolution'* in 1939, as well as many other books and articles. Another of his well-known books was a biography of the historian Tacitus, which was published in 1958. He was referred to as "(the) greatest of modern historians on ancient Rome." As just stated, the *reason* for this is the fact that he was an Inner-Circle member. But like many I.C. members, he kept his knowledge about the actual truth of history to himself and put the things that he knew about, in his work in a way that would be accepted by his peers. He also understood that the vast majority of scholars of his day were really quite sad by comparison, that they really lacked the discipline that would have allowed them to advance to his level of scholarship.

It was Anthony Birley who had edited Syme's *'Roman Papers'*, vol. III-VII, and his *'Anatolica'* (studies on Strabo on ancient Turkey). Birley has been cited at times before, with regards to items which relate to this subject, as he is the author of many books on ancient Rome. Anthony Birley is professor of Ancient History at the University of Dusseldorf, and he was previously professor of Ancient History at the University of Manchester. We have to wonder if Syme had entrusted the knowledge that he had, with anyone else and who those persons might be. One possible candidate might be G.W. Bowersock, who is a modern Roman historian and a pupil of Sir Ronald Syme. We also wonder if Syme had left any I.C. notes in his own personal files and if they were found by anyone.

BACKGROUND

THE NEW CLASSICAL SCHOLARSHIP

One of the main things that people, who begin the study of this subject, should be made aware of is, that we have termed ourselves the 'New Classical Scholarship' as opposed to the 'Old Classical Scholarship'. Another thing that we should discuss are those whom we term the 'Transitory Classical Scholarship'. For each of these we use the terms 'N.C.S.', 'O.C.S', and 'T.C.S.' respectively.

In examinations which have been made regarding this subject, we have isolated what we refer to as the Six Major Assumptions made by the O.C.S. (The Old Classical Scholarship), which are: they assume that the ancient authors

(1) of history were who they claimed to be.

(2) were writing in an honest and forthright manner.

(3) did not use hidden agendas or ulterior motives for misleading the reader, or listeners.

(4) were not closely related to each other and therefore, were not writing in concert with each other.

(5) were not writing from within a "controlled environment" where only certain people could write for public consumption. (Meaning royals only, no matter how it would "appear" that a measure of freedom of speech existed in those times.)

(6) were not using literary devices and other methods in which to deliberately deceive the masses.

But, there are other facades or illusions which were also created and used to prevent the general public from discovering the truth about ancient history; all of which will remain hidden from anyone who does not research the subject properly. "Convention" is what the Old Classical Scholarship assumes most of all, and what prevents those who research in that way from ever finding the truth in and about ancient history. Before we get into some of those other things, we need to discuss the major differences between the Old Classical Scholarship and the New Classical Scholarship.

The problem with the conventional methods that are used by the O.C.S. relating to the study of ancient history is, that it assumes too much. Firstly, conventional methods would only be valid if ancient history (or any other history for that matter) were "conventional." In other words, you would be accepting at face value the histories of that time and whatever the historians have written, as being true, virtually without question. Why? Because that is what 'convention' demands. It assumes that there were regulations in place as if those histories were written within a society like our own today. It assumes freedom of speech and, that the authors were not only honest, but they were also actually whom they claimed they were, which is not completely true.

If what you are examining is not properly scrutinized, then you are not going to get to the truth of the matter. The research of ancient history needs to be conducted by gathering information using various methods and means; logically, from sources within a specific time for comparison and examination. The data should be statistical and allows construction of an actual model of the contextual reality involved. This is done so that one is aware of just what they are working with in terms of intellect and literary ability of the authors. This is how one should make determinations – by having before them actual instances and components to work with, showing precedent examples displayed by each author. Such things can never be achieved by making conventional assumptions.

Secondly, for the conventional methods used by the Old Classical Scholarship to work, the assumption must be made that the historians were not lying and not deliberately misleading the reader. In our research, we have discovered that these ancient authors were, a) closely related to each other, b) were either royalty or close relatives of the ruling royals, c) used alias names for specific purposes (to hide their true identity and to make it appear that many more people were writing than actually were), as well as for several other reasons which the conventional O.C.S. have never discovered.

This research is like discovering that extremely well-educated pirates were in total control of the Roman Empire when Christianity was being made, as they left hints and clues about the locations of their (literary) treasures, much like we know of pirates doing.

We also have concerns about the O.C.S. promoting what is referred to as 'parroting'. The O.C.S. insists upon citation of each and every item. But, when it is discovered that the proper way of examining ancient history is really 100 times more complicated than the way that the O. C. S. has been doing it, such things become impossible for individuals to do within one short lifetime. The concern with this is more of an immediate one. That is, if one gives specific and detailed references to each and every thing spoken of, this will lead to laziness on the part of those who are researching the subject. If one only looks to the items that are cited, they are not exposed to the total overall picture which is only gained by reading and familiarizing one's self with the histories of the time in question. If a person is continually reading those histories in an ongoing manner, they will know where the passages are which are being referred to without having specific citations for all of them.

Another reason for actually reading through all of these histories as opposed to 'cheating' is because this is the only way that the researcher will ever be able to make progress and discover even more items which relate to the subject. The difference being that in the one case the person is simply reading the work that has already been done and probably referring to certain passages which have been cited. That does not give the person an actual knowledge or understanding of the true context of ancient history or how the things being spoken of actually 'fit' into that time. But the person who has a working knowledge of the ancient history in question, will see and understand much more and, will be able to contribute something of value to the research itself. Again, this is the only way that progress will be made – if people do not take the lazy way out that has been taught by the Old Classical Scholarship. These are some of the differences between the Old Classical Scholarship and the New Classical Scholarship.

In the New Classical Scholarship, we realize that we must think in the same ways that great detectives would. We must become great detectives ourselves, following every clue no matter how small or unimportant they may appear when we first notice them. We must approach this (ancient history and the truth about the invention of Christianity) as a great mystery waiting to be solved and unraveled to learn who invented it, why and how they achieved their goal.

Therefore, we cannot afford to do this research with eyes closed and just believing and accepting, nor limit ourselves to methods of convention, as doing so causes presumption of that which may not be true. This is a point that we will have to make understood to those who are presently a part of academia. They have learned and use methods that are incorrect and which restrict what the conclusions are that they may reach and for the most part they are unaware of this fact. Scholars and researchers cannot, we must not, presume that ancient history was written with the same convention that we are familiar with today. The times we refer to, were different in a number of ways and should be viewed from that perspective, and not as you might be tempted to view it; by simply reading and accepting all of it as being true.

We must start from an objective and unbiased standpoint, using every logical and critical method as well as every viable means available. Ancient literature must not only be read, but broken down and analyzed as literature in all its various component parts. That is how we gain the data to begin making a true assessment of the situation. When that it done, one will have the basis with which to proceed in a critical examination and will finally be able to discover (or uncover) the truth.

Some of you who are reading this may already know, those whom we term 'Transitory Classical Scholars' are those who have done work which is very much like our own, but whom have not yet discovered what we have. They are, if they stay the course, "on the way" to understanding what we of the 'N.C.S.' already know. Nevertheless, those who are of the T.C.S. still currently do not understand what we do, or if they do, they are not writing about it as we are. There are numerous people who fall into this category and many of them are popular and familiar scholars who have written several well-received books. One of those whom we refer to as a 'T.C.S.' wrote a book titled *'Gospel Fictions'*. Another one who may be termed a 'T.C.S.' is the author of a book titled *'First Century Judaism in Crisis'*. Therefore, you may know of some of these scholars. For more about this see the book *'The Synthesis of Christianity'*.

A BACKGROUND HISTORY OF THE NEW CLASSICAL SCHOLARSHIP

Where did it start? We generally go back to Bruno Bauer as being the very first person to write publicly on his research about examining the New Testament texts as literature; although, there were others before him who had touched upon the subject. Bruno Bauer had put forth the most comprehensive study of the subject, arriving at conclusions which were the most specific, concise, pointing out what so many others had missed - it was the Romans who invented and wrote the New Testament!

There has also been a rumor circulating on the Internet which I, Roman Piso, have addressed several times. Someone had invented a rumor about when and where the idea of the 'Piso Theory' started. When people resort to inventing rumors, this demonstrates their frustration with the issue. Someone had the bright idea of putting forth the rumor that this research was all a hoax created by students at a University, I think they were saying that it started at UC Berkeley. There isn't any problem mentioning this, because people ought to know that this rumor exists and there are bound to be others as well. This is the sort of dishonest tactics that certain persons, groups, and various organizations resort to, and more, in attempting to prevent the truth becoming known by the general public.

This is the reason for taking the time to present the real progression of this study and show how it is that we have gotten to this point from those original researchers. It was Bruno Bauer's work which first pointed people in the right direction, by emphasizing two very important things; a) the importance of objective study and research, b) the importance of examining ancient texts as literature, and c) the conclusion of the facts and data gained by his work demonstrated Roman involvement in the making of the Christian religion and the authorship of the New Testament texts.

There were others who wrote on this subject. They went unheeded by academia for the most part. One such person was James Ballantyne Hannay. He was a British scholar who also wrote about the Romans inventing Christianity. There is mention about the work of Hannay and of others, in other books we are working on, and mention of him at times in this book. His book was published right after he died, and consequently he never got to see a copy of it. After his death in 1925, there really weren't any serious researchers for many years, that we know of, which detailed the Roman involvement in the making of the Christian religion. This is partly due to WWII escalating shortly after that time, and his book was apparently put out in a very limited printing, leaving most scholars unaware of his work.

In 1979, Abelard Reuchlin had put his research into a comprehensive form by publishing a booklet titled *'The True Authorship Of The New Testament'*. It is this booklet which had informed many thousands of people over the years as to the truth regarding the Roman invention and writing of the New Testament story. Several others worldwide have written on this subject since that time. There were a number of people in the 1980's who were bringing up this subject in their own books. One such person was Dr. W. F. Dean. He wrote a book *('The Mania of Religion')*, which includes several areas that mention the Piso family involvement in the invention of the Christian religion and writing the New Testament story. You will be able to find more information about these and other authors in the Bibliography section of this book.

THE TERMS 'ALLY' AND 'AXIS' AS DESIGNATORS

We are defining new territory and cannot in the least be afraid to use new, different and unique ideas and to apply existing ideas, or that which has already been established elsewhere in order to help others better understand details we present. Also, we need to enlist aids if necessary, as this is just too important to pass up those opportunities as and when they present themselves to us. An example of this would be the use of the words 'Ally' and 'Axis' as designators. These designators help us to categorize those who were on the side of good (who had good intent, good goals, and who may even have given their lives for that good) and those who were not.

These are the same designators used by those examining WWII and which helped people define just which nations were on which side in that war. Although we did not apply these designators strictly for identifying 'nations' in our study of the great, long all-out war between the Romans and the Jews, which was the reason for the New Testament being written and the invention of the Christian religion. We extended the use of these designators to include individuals, so that we can show more clearly who had specific motives, and to expose the truth about this subject with the necessary specifics as required in this strict discipline. This is how the history of the time referred to here, will be seen from now and on into the future. Scholars will be viewing everyone of that time in history, who in the Roman Empire or who interacted with it, as being in or of either of these two camps; Ally or Axis. This is a process that we researchers have been working on for some time now, but which even at this late date has yet to be made a general practice among scholars and researchers of that time in history.

Everything from those times need to be re-evaluated and the persons who lived then and played a part in the history as it was recorded, need to be shown as they really were; on one side of that long all-out war, or the other. This is the only way that we will ever have the genuine truth of the subject, and it is what we owe to those who gave their lives so that we might one day know the truth of it all. There are, until this time, unknown and unsung heroes that deserve to be acknowledged for all that they did and gave for the sake of humanity. In this we see the grave importance of doing this research as it should be done. It is time now to look boldly at the reality of what actually happened in those times, and face the truth which has been so long ignored; which is, that those who were writing those histories and holy books lied to us; the people of the world.

For all of the reasons that we have ever given why this new view of ancient history should be known and observed, we suggest that it be for three or four of the most important of those reasons. And those are; (1) because of, and for all of those who died so that we might be able to figure it all out one day and be free of the lies, and (2) so that we can have truth known once and for all, so that everyone will know it and (3) to take away the division that was created by those lies, so that the world may be united by the truth, rather than divided by lies. The world has never known or even been able to think upon all that might have been if only things had been different back in the time of that great ancient war. Add a fourth reason to the list of why this is so extremely important, and that would be because we, humanity, cannot afford to ever allow what happened then to happen again. The fourth reason would be so that we (the human race) can learn this most valuable lesson and never forget it. That is just the most basic and essential reasons for taking heed of this research.

Tacitus provides us, by bits and pieces here and there, with valuable information about the war that was raging while the Romans were writing the New Testament text and building Christianity. He, along with other writers of his time, supply us with information about just who was on which side of the war. Therefore, to point out designated individuals in their respective positions during that war, we use the terms 'Axis' and 'Allies'. Those who were with the Pisos are referred to as the 'Axis' and, those who were allied with the Pharisees are designated as 'Allies'.

For your edification, before we proceed in this examination of the 'Histories' of Tacitus, we will mention for you some of the Roman xxviii | Piso Christ

Emperors and the side they were on in the war of the Pisos against the Pharisees; Nero was an Ally, Galba and Licinianus Frugi Piso were of the Axis, Otho is a bit of a puzzle and there is a lot of confusing information. Perhaps Otho was really out for himself, although there was at least the pretense of being an 'Ally'. However, when considering that Vitellius could not stand for Otho to be Emperor, it appears that Otho was actually on the side of the Axis.

Vitellius was an Ally of the Pharisees as he actually did some things to show himself to be such; for example, he was a champion of the slaves and common people by rallying them together to fight the adversity to their freedom. Vitellius was killed by Arrius Piso (using in history, the name of Antonius Primus). Knowing just who was an 'Ally' and who was a member of the 'Axis' is the key to understanding why each did certain things during their lives and, for some also during their rule. As one can observe, the particular role of each of these persons in their position as either an 'Ally' or being one of the 'Axis' is consistent throughout – and because of this, it indeed serves as a proof of the position taken by each person involved.

"The (Roman) armies in Germany at the time were unhappy, worried and angry, which causes a condition most dangerous when large forces are involved. They were moved by pride in their recent victory, and also by fear out of concern because they had favored the losing side. They had been slow to abandon Nero; and Verginius (Rufus), their commander, had not pronounced (support) for Galba immediately; men were inclined to think that Verginius Rufus would not be unwilling to be emperor himself. It was believed that the soldiers offered support for him to gain the imperial power." This is important, as it allows us to know that Verginius Rufus was a person who might have come close to becoming emperor of Rome.

"The East was as yet undisturbed. Syria and four Roman legions were held under command of Licinius Mucianus, a man notorious in prosperity and adversity alike. When a young man he had cultivated friendships with the nobility for his own gain; later, when his wealth was exhausted, his position insecure, and he also suspected that Claudius was angry with him, he withdrew to retirement in Asia and was as near to exile then as he was later to the throne of Rome." This represents an indication that Licinius Mucianus had also come close to becoming emperor! Tactius goes on to say about him; "… he was a man who found it easier to bestow the imperial power than to hold it himself."

In the footnotes of the Loeb Classical Library edition of Tacitus' 'Histories', there is this commentary; "Licinius Mucianus had been consul under Nero, and in 67 (C.E.) was appointed governor of Syria. After Vespasian claimed the imperial power, Mucianus became his strongest supporter..." Now we read; "Neither Vespasian's desires nor sentiments were opposed to Galba, for he sent his son, Titus, to pay his respects to Galba to show his allegiance to him, as we shall explain at the proper time." Naturally, this is because both Galba and Vespasian, along with Vespasian's son Titus, were of the 'Axis'.

There is much to think about and because of having now started the use of the designators 'Axis' and 'Allies' we will now find it much easier to identify each individual in their respective role as either one of these. To make it easier, we might well think of the 'Allies' as the good guys, while the 'Axis' would represent the bad guys, the people who were building and promoting Christianity.

CHAPTER I

THE PISO FAMILY

ARRIUS PISO AS DIO CHRYSOSTOM (aka Dio Cocceianus Chrysostom of Prusa)

As Dio Chrysostom, Arrius Piso appeared as a Greek orator (Arrius Piso's main language was Greek) and philosopher (which is also what Arrius Piso was or considered himself to be), who was banished from Rome by Emperor Domitian (younger brother of Titus). He returned to Rome when Domitian died and was welcomed back by Emperor Nerva. Arrius Piso was supposed to have had many adventures while in exile, and he and Pliny the Younger saw each other in Prusa, Bithynia, as Pliny had went to see him in Prusa (Ref. Pliny the Younger, 'Epistles').

Now, we will examine some of the facts given about Dio Chrysostom. There is never a definite date given for either his birth or death, only an estimate. This is a clue that Dio Chrysostom was actually an alias. He is said to have been born in Prusa, of Bithynia about the year 40 C.E. And, he is supposed to have died around 120 C.E. This mirrors Arrius Piso's birth and death; Arrius was born in 37 C.E. and died in 119 C.E.

In the name Dio Chrysostom, 'Dio' means 'God', and as Jesus, Arrius Piso was playing God, and we also have a variation of 'Christ' in the name 'Chrys(t)ostom'. Another thing is that 'Chrysostom' means (the) 'golden mouthed'. If anyone ever was golden mouthed (because all that came out of his mouth was 'gold'), it was Arrius Piso. This also points to him being Flavius ('golden') Josephus. This is how they gave a confirmation about being correct in following the clues that they give; they made certain that there were several indications that urge you to find, with certainty, exactly what they meant because when you do uncover the actual meaning of their clues, it all fits together like pieces of a puzzle.

We find that Arria the Younger and Fannia* were banished from Rome, but we do not find in superficial history what has become of Arrius Piso during this time. Since we do not find anything, we are lead to believe that he is still in Rome and living and working with Emperor Titus. However, further research leads to finding Arrius Piso secretly co-ruling with Titus and that he was also calling himself Titus during that time.

Furthermore, Titus and Arrius Piso had married women who were sisters, making Titus and Arrius Piso brothers-in-law. All of this done, apparently with the blessing of Vespasian (Titus' father), who was still alive at the time. Next, we discover just what happened when we realize that Arrius Piso was Dio Chrysostom because as Dio Chrysostom, that information is given. Obviously, Arria the Younger and Fannia were NOT under banishment while either Vespasian or Titus lived. Vespasian and Titus both were friendly to them. They hadn't any reason to 'rid Rome' of them. This too, is another clue.

We then find that as Dio Chrysostom, Arrius Piso himself, was banished in the year 82 C.E. This is shortly after Domitian becomes emperor. Knowing that Domitian and Arrius Piso did not get along, and that Domitian was not about to co-rule with Arrius Piso as his brother Titus had, he had Arrius Piso and his family exiled. To where were they exiled? To Prusa, in Bithynia. As already mentioned, Dio Chrysostom was welcomed back to Rome AFTER Domitian was killed, and Dio Chrysostom is recorded as being a good and close friend of the emperor Trajan. And why would he be a close friend to Emperor Trajan? He, Dio Chrysotom, was really Arrius Piso, Trajan's father-in-law!**

Other information about Dio Chrysostom is that he was involved in an urban renewal lawsuit to beautify the city of Prusa in the year 111 C.E. Now knowing that Dio is really Arrius Piso using the alias of Dio Chrysotom, this tells us that Arrius Piso lived beyond the year 111 C.E., which is something that we already knew because of other evidence. Arrius Piso, writing as Dio Chrysostom, paralleled the 'teachings' and verses of the New Testament just as Seneca (a relative of Arrius Piso on his mother's side) had done earlier*** and in his (Arrius Piso) exile acted (supposedly) similarly to how his invented Jesus was supposed to have acted, including living "humbly" and philosophizing.

Now, looking back to what Abelard Reuchlin says about Arrius Piso under another alias. He says; "As Claudius Aristion (form of Aristo), Arrius

Piso was the leading citizen of Ephesus. That was the chief city of the province of Asia, located southwest of Bithynia. As (Flavius) Archippus, the philosopher, Piso had been honored by Emperor Domitian; the emperor "commended" him to Pliny the Younger (Lappius Maximus, an alias used by Pliny) in Bithynia, and ordered Pliny (Terentius Maximus, another Pliny alias) to buy him (Flavius Archippus –actually Arrius Piso) a farm near Prusa. And the people of Prusa voted him as Archippus, a statue."****

If one reads about Domitian's rule, it is clear that he was worried and extremely troubled in his rule. He seemed to be expecting to be killed at any time. He knew very well that having exiled Arrius Piso and his family, he was asking for trouble and he knew that Arrius Piso had killed emperors before, and had others killed by persons he trusted or coerced. This was not an apparently 'good will' gesture by Domitian to Arrius Piso. He was simply trying to (placate) get on the good side of Arrius Piso, as if there were such a thing. Domitian knew that Arrius Piso had Nero killed (by using Epaphroditus, Nero's personal scribe), and Piso had the "privilege" of personally killing the emperor Vitellius (while he, Arrius Piso used the alias Antonius Primus).*****

These facts were well known to Domitian. So, though Domitian was opposed to co-rule with Arrius Piso as did his brother Titus, Domitian was nonetheless frightened of Arrius Piso and did whatever he could, within the circumstances, to appease him.

There is something that Dio Chrysostom (Arrius Piso) was apparently grumbling about, which reveals more than one might notice at first (as mentioned in Reuchlin's 'The True Authorship of the New Testament', pg. 16),. This is the line that states; "… surely you have noticed what some of our booksellers do? …Because they, knowing that old books are in demand since better written and on better paper, bury the worst specimens of our day in grain in order that they may take on the same color as the old ones, and after ruining the books into the bargain they sell them as old." The line indicates this was really quite fitting of being said by Arrius Piso. The reason? Because, as already revealed herein, Arrius Piso also wrote as Philo, and he was hinting at this, by saying that because what he was doing was actually 'covering his own guilt'. Why? Because Arrius Piso was the person burying books in grain to make them appear to be older books.

In addition, had Arrius Piso not written under the alias "Philo", and gave another example of a Jew writing in Greek, he and the work he produced, using the alias "Flavius Josephus" would have stuck out like a sore thumb! Writing as Josephus, he knew this and did the very same thing with Philo as he did with Jesus; he historicized him to make him appear to be a real person! And then there is the 'Logos' connection between Philo and the New Testament. It was Arrius Piso using the alias "Philo" who gave his view about there being only 'two races of men'. And by that he meant royal and non-royal.

* Arria the Younger was Arrius Piso's mother and Fannia (Flavia Arria) was Arrius Piso's sister. You can find their banishment recorded superficially in history.

** Trajan was married to Claudia Phoebe aka Pompeia Plotina, daughter of Arrius Piso.

*** Arrius Piso also wrote as Plutarch, in which his major work was titled "Parallel Lives." That he had paralleled Seneca as Dio Chrysostom is another indication that Dio Chrysostom was actually Arrius Piso.

**** The reference for this is in 'The True Authorship of the New Testament', by Abelard Reuchlin, under 'The Creation of the Church', pages 15 and 16. Also there, he says; "Dio Chrysostom, Bithynian orator and philosopher, addressed the city assembly of this same Prusa in Bithynia, lauding Diodorus – but with unclear meanings. Diodorus meant the gift of god, by which Dio means Piso!" Yes, and it was really Arrius Piso calling himself as what he saw himself to be; a gift of god! Since he saw himself as god, he was saying that he was his own gift! He was praising himself for all he had done and that he had still planned to do!

***** That Arrius Piso (using the alias "Antonius Primus") personally killed Vitellius, is recorded by Suetonius in 'The Twelve Caesars', under 'Vitellius'.

THE PISOS, FLAVIANS & BALBI

To better understand what was happening in the first century C.E. (common era or current era), and how power over all of the Roman Empire came into the hands of the Flavians, one needs to examine all who supported their rise to Imperial power – including their royal relatives. A few years ago, something about the discovery of a stone tablet, was being mentioned, on which had information about the Piso family. It is very likely that more than just one such tablet has been discovered. This one tablet, referred to the Gneius Calpurnius Piso who poisoned Germanicus Caesar in 19 C.E. There was quite a bit of information on that tablet (or set of tablets?). It seems that it was a tablet which gave the details of the trial of Gneius Piso in regards to the deed of which he was accused (poisoning Germanicus). However, the real value to those of us who are piecing together the family tree of the Pisos and their relatives is the genealogical information which was given on that tablet.

The tablet confirms a marriage between the Piso and the Balbii families. This information actually completes a circle of involvement and connections between the Pisos, the Flavians and the Balbi. The Balbii were financial backers and supporters of Vespasian in his bid for the Imperial throne of Rome. We know of the marriage of Julius Caesar to one of the Piso women (Calpurnia, the daughter of Lucius Calpurnius Piso Caesoninus, the consul of 58 B.C.E.); (Before Current Era); but his son, is the Lucius Calpurnius Piso (Caesoninus) who was a pontifex, and consul in the year 15 C.E., was the father of another Calpurnia – and it is this Calpurnia who married Lucius Nonius (Atius) Balbus Asperinas, who was a consul in the year 6 C.E. This Lucius Nonius (Atius) Balbus Asperinas fits into the puzzle to be the grandson of that Marcus Nonius Atius Balbus who circa 30 B.C.E., married Julia (Minor), the sister of the dictator Julius Caesar.

This is a truly complicated family tree with very closely knitted relationships between royals. Also, this Lucius Nonius (Atius) Balbus (Asperinas) was the nephew of Atia (Major) who was married to Augustus Caesar! There are other later relationships between these families that will better clarify the motives for the things which we have been examining, as to the making of the New Testament (the Jesus story).

Lucius Nonius (Atius) Balbus (Asperinas) was involved in establishing a line of royal relatives which would come to spawn major players in the power game of the year 68 C.E. He fathered a son who married a noble woman named Viciria. Born to Viciria and her husband was a son named Marcus Nonius (Atius) Balbus (Sr.). He and his son Marcus Nonius (Atius) Balbus (Jr.) were major supporters of Vespasian during that critical time, just before Vespasian became Emperor of Rome. They lived near the Piso family villa at Herculaneum, and their home too, was buried when Mount Vesuvius erupted in 79 C.E. That is how we know most of what we do about them.

Marcus Nonius Atius Balbus (Sr.) was married to one Volasennia, and had at least three children that we know of; a son (Marcus Nonius Atius Balbus (Jr.), and two daughters. The father and son team of Marcus Nonius Atius Balbus (Sr.) and Marcus Nonius Atius Balbus (Jr.) of circa 68 C.E. apparently were also involved in the Pisos' conspiracy against Nero, as well as helping to put down the rivals of Vespasian in his pursuit of the Imperial power. Those of you who have been researching this subject may know, that the key person in the invention and writing of the New Testament was Arrius Calpurnius Piso aka Flavius Josephus, and he was a great nephew of the Emperor Vespasian by way of Vespasian's brother, T. Flavius Sabinus whose wife was Arria the Elder. Arrius Calpurnius Piso was the son of Arria the Younger, who was the daughter of Arria the Elder. There wasn't any need to claim Josephus/Arrius Piso as having been adopted by Vespasian, other than to be used as another way to hide behind the alias of Flavius Josephus. Here we have laid out some relationships, and perhaps these are beginning to show the reader how the royals were connected and to whom, and why they were so powerful.

In his *"Vita,"* Flavius Josephus' (actually Arrius Calpurnius Piso) great-grandfather was called Simon 'Psellus,'* which means 'stutterer.' If you take the information that we have and trace his ancestry back and concentrate on his great-grandfathers, you will find that a piece of the puzzle fits!** Arrius Piso did have a great-grandfather whose name means 'stutterer,' but it is not 'Psellus,' but Balbus! And this is because Balbus also means stutterer!*** This great-grandfather is the father of Arrius Piso's grandmother, and we discovered that her name of 'Munatia' is really 'Nonia' (that is, with 'mun' as 'nun'/'non' phonetically) Atia. Knowing this reveals her as a Balbii. She is the daughter of Plancinas Munatius, the wife of Gneius Calpurnius Piso, whom we have already discussed above. ****

Notes & References:

* Ref. The first verse of the Vita ('Life of Flavius Josephus'), Loeb Classical Library Edition of the works of Flavius Josephus and/or Whiston's English translation.

** Also note that the Gneius Calpurnius Piso who poisoned Germanicus Caesar in 19 C.E., apparently had been married to a woman who appears in history as Plancina Munatia. If one views her name in the royal language, the Munatia part of her name changes to 'Non-Atia,' which is Nonia Atia. If this is really her name it infers that she too was of Balbii origin. The reason being two-fold; (1) 'Nonia' is a known name of the Balbii women. (2) 'Atia' infers Balbii. Also since we were deliberately led to find this because of the statements made by Arrius Piso writing as Flavius Josephus, and because it fits into the puzzle, the likelihood is such that we should accept this and see if more determining factors can be found.

*** Ref. The works of Flavius Josephus, Loeb Classical Library Edition, footnote to the first verse of the Vita ('Life of Flavius Josephus'). One may also want to note that the Loeb Classical Library Edition of Flavius Josephus has a comprehensive Index at the end of the last volume.

**** This does, however, also mean that we must investigate just who Plancinas Munatius really was... meaning, just which Balbii.

The Introduction to Pliny the Younger's Letters and Panagericus, Book I, page xiv (Loeb Classical Library Edition). This gives a genealogy of the line involving Arria the Elder and Arria the Younger.

"Herculaneum: Italy's Buried Treasure," Joseph Jay Deiss, Harper & Row, 1985. This gives information on the villas found at Herculaneum regarding the Pisos & Balbii.

"Nero, the end of a Dynasty," Griffen. Piso family information.

"Senatus Consultum de Cn. Pisone" (This refers to the tablet which was mentioned above).

"A Historical Commentary on Tacitus' Histories I and II," Guy Edward F. Chilver, Claridon Press, Oxford, 1979, pg. 74. Information on the Piso family tree.

"From Tiberius to the Antonines (A.D. 14 - 192)," by Albino Garzetti, pub. Methuen, London, 1974: Distributed in the U.S. by Harper & Row, Barnes & Noble.

"Dio Cassius," Loeb Classical Library Edition, (LXVIII, 3,2). Piso family relations.

Below is a link to a very scholarly genealogy of the Piso family which shows some of the marriages between the Pisos and other royal houses; particularly, those mentioned above.

http://perso.wanadoo.fr/publie/pison/caeso.htm

Gneius (Gnaeus) Calpurnius Piso, the husband of Plancina Munatia was consul in the year 7 B.C.E. Studying Arrius Piso's ancestry back through his father's mother (Plancina Munatia), to her father as Arrius Piso's maternal great-grandfather, and if her name indicates that her father was a Balbii, then Arrius Piso's statement (in his Vita), writing as Flavius Josephus, of his great-grandfather having the name 'Psellus' (stutterer) is found to be correct as Balbi also means "stutterer." One may also wish to note that this great-grandfather of Arrius Piso (Plancinas Munatius) can be found under that name in history. So, as with our process of finding out who other alias names belong to, we must do the same thing in this instance by creating a profile utilizing all known data regarding Plancina Munatius. Marcus Nonius Atius Balbus Sr. (c. 68 C.E.) was proconsul of Crete and Cyrenaica; a Roman colony in North Africa.

SOME PISO FAMILY RELATIVES

The Atii Balbii are royal relatives of the Piso family. The Balbii family intermarried with the Piso family. One confirmed marriage between the two families has been found. Perhaps at a later date a detailed treatise can be given on the Balbii family. That family also supported Vespasian (there is the link between the Pisos and the Flavians, via the Balbii) financially, helping to secure Vespasian's position as Emperor.

The Balbii family were also neighbors of the Pisos at Herculaneum, and had a villa of their own close to that of the Pisos. To research this you will want to read *"Herculaneum: Italy's Buried Treasure,"* a book by Joseph Jay Deiss. It is a major source of information for the facts regarding Atii Balbii.

THE ANNII VERI

The Annii Veri(i) are generally considered the family that derived from a great-grandfather of the Emperor Marcus Aurelius. This great-grandfather of Marcus Aurelius was also the grandfather of Annia Galeria Faustina I, wife of Emperor Antoninus Pius. In *"Marcus Aurelius, A Biography,"* by Birley, published at Yale, circa 1986, there is a genealogy chart given for the Annii Veri(i). It is informative as it mentions "Annius Verus" of Ucubi as the common ancestor of the Annii Verii. This person is undoubtedly Arrius Piso using the alias 'Annius Verus'. He is simply being called Annius (changed from 'Arrius'), with "Veri," which is the Roman version of the Egyptian 'Veru,' meaning "wise man" or in the plural, "wise men." This could have been associated with the "wise men" who had come from the East as mentioned in the Jesus story. Birley's chart is helpful, but it is only when one is able to further identify those listed in it, that a greater clarification is acquired.

THE ANNII ANICI

The Annii Anici(i) emerged as prominent Romans in the later Roman Empire, but they too, just as the Annii Verii, were descendants of Arrius Piso. Just as there was an explanation for the name Annii Veri, there is also one for the Annii Anici name. The "Anni" part of the name is there to show the commonality with the Annii Veri, showing the same source, i.e., having the same common ancestor (Arrius Piso).

And the "Anicii" part of the name is "A" as an acrostic initial. While the "Nici" portion is secretly Nic(on) meaning 'Victor,' and which is an abbreviation for 'Nicomachus,' another alias name used by Arrius Piso, referring to him as "the victor of the battle (of Garaza)." He was the winner of the battle of Garaza against the Jews (showing that Arrius Piso was a General in the Roman army fighting AGAINST the Jews, and not a JEWISH General as he claimed under the name of Flavius Josephus).

Some of the Anici boldly joked about this (further confirming the facts just stated), by naming their sons "Nicomachus." Instances include: Amnius Manlius Nicomachus Anicius Paulinus, and Marcus Junius Caesonius Nicomachus Anicius Faustus. Note that the "A" as an acrostic initial could be any number of his alias names by Arrius Piso that begin with 'A'. These would include "Antonius" (with 'Primus' inferred), or "Antoninus," which would make "Arrius Antoninus," with the Nicomachus name. Meaning that these names represented the same person.

THE GREGORIES

Abelard Reuchlin says that the Annii Anicii later became the persons in history using the name "Gregory." This area has not yet been explored in the same way that Reuchlin has, and he is thought to be correct, at least to the extent that a branch or branches of the Annii Anicii later became the families producing those powerful "Gregories" or Gregorians. As we go on in our research, we will get into more of the details about these. .

PROFILES OF ARRIUS PISO & HIS FAMILY

The first source that we look to for information on Arrius Piso and his family is in the work done on this subject by Abelard Reuchlin ("The True Authorship of the New Testament").This is the very first work that actually talks about Arrius Calpurnius Piso and his family as the authors of the New Testament.

One thing that should be noted is, (as of this writing) Abelard Reuchlin has corrected the few things in his work which were incorrect for whatever reason (typos/misquotes, or etc). One of the main things was that he had mentioned Lucius Calpurnius Piso as Arrius Piso's father. He had learned this to be incorrect in the mid 1980's when he discovered the work of Guy Edward Farquar Chilver on the works of Tacitus. There, he realized that Gaius Calpurnius Piso – who was sentenced to death by Nero, was the father of Arrius Piso (full name, Arrius Calpurnius Piso). (Note that Reuchlin still has not corrected the information in his booklet and does not plan to do so. Instead, he is working on a new, more advanced and informational work to be completed in several volumes).

Abelard Reuchlin, in his booklet, "The True Authorship of the New Testament" gives the various Piso family alias names and tells us just who were the immediate family members. Namely, Arrius Piso's sons and his daughter Claudia Phoebe/Pompeia Plotina. He tells us of Arrius Piso's four sons, Alexander, Julius, Justus and Proculus Piso, and some things about their children (the grand-children of Arrius Piso). Reuchlin tells us how one may find where he obtained this information, citing the *Vita* of Flavius Josephus.

In the *Vita*, you can find that information along with the birth dates for three of Arrius Piso' sons. Furthermore, in the Vita of Flavius Josephus (Arrius Piso), one also can find that under the name of Flavius Josephus, Arrius Piso was married three times. This is actually quite a bit of information, and it is amazing to think of just how many so-called scholars over the course of so many hundred years have overlooked this and never put any of this together as did Reuchlin..

More amazing is that Josephus (Arrius Piso) makes it so easy to learn the age of each of three of his sons by giving their births by particular times during the reigns of emperors. With this information, we know the following, that (1) Arrius Piso was married three times, (2) at the time that he wrote the Vita he had three living sons (because Alexander (the eldest son) was then dead, and there was his daughter Claudia). (3) He did not have any children by his first wife, (4) by further deduction, we find that Alexander and his brother Julius Piso both had the same mother, and (5) their mother was Arrius Piso's second wife, Boionia Priscilla, (6) brothers Justus and Proculus Piso had the same mother, and she was Arrius Piso's third wife, (7) it now appears that Claudia Phoebe's mother was also Boionia Priscilla, Arrius Piso's second wife.

As for the dates when his sons and daughter were born, we find those as;

> [C. , is for Calpurnius, the clan or family middle name]
> Alexander C. Piso, born between 71-73 C.E. (died circa 95 C.E.)
> Julius C. Piso, born 74 C.E. (died in 138 C.E.)
> Claudia Phoebe, born before 77 C.E. (died 129 C.E. as Pompeia Plotina)
> Justus C. Piso, born 77 C.E. (died after 140 C.E.)
> Proculus C. Piso, born 79 C.E. (died after 115 C.E.)

Currently, there is a problem with determining the parentage of Arrius Piso's second wife, Boionia Priscilla This problem came about when we found the authors of that history created the problem deliberately by making it appear that there were two brothers with similar names... when at the same time, it may well be that instead of brothers having similar names that this may be a case of ONE person with modified names. However, we do know the name of Boionia Priscilla's father and can work from there. (Old notes show him listed as Boreas Soranus) and the authors of the history of that time make it appear that he had a brother who had a similar name but whose name was 'Sura' instead of Soranus. This is the usual type of corruption that we find in researching ancient history. (This being the case, we also run into the possibility of other items being inferred, which will have to be commented upon and explained in other books).

Arrius Piso's third wife is described as a Jewess who had been living at Crete. She, as has been said, was the mother of Justus C. Piso and Proculus C. Piso. Interestingly enough (since we see Proculus' mother as a Jewess), we see that one of Proculus Piso's alias names as 'Agrippa'... a patently Jewish name. Note that our further research reveals that the mother of Arrius Piso's two youngest children, Justus and Proculus, was actually Berenice, the sister of Agrippa II. We will get into this in much more detail in other examinations of this topic.

One must keep in mind while thinking of this, that what has been learned from this is, there were very few people who were in control of so much of the world during that time of the Roman Empire. Only a few royals who out-ranked other royals within the Roman Empire, and in turn the out-ranked royals ruled over and controlled the masses of the Empire. This meant that for the royals to keep their power, the common people had to be completely kept in ignorance about the reality of using many alias names and who actually were the few persons who were doing so many things. No one other than those who were in control could write books that would ever be distributed widely throughout the Roman Empire. In this way those in control could create an illusion by writing books. A part of the deception was the use of pennames or alias identities. The reason for this was to create the illusion that many different persons were writing but, actually only few persons were actually writing. Doing so meant that the masses would think there was a measure of 'freedom' that allowed many to be able to write and get their message out to other people of the Empire - in reality, such freedom did not exist. There wasn't anything such as freedom of speech as we know it to be in the time that we now live.

Arrius Piso and his close relatives went about writing under various alias names, creating and spreading this illusion. His sons too, were actively writing to help make this illusion seem real, as did his grandsons too, who wrote and helped create this façade. Arrius Piso also writing under many alias names, played many characters in history and in the biblical texts that they were writing. His son Justus Piso wrote as Justin Martyr. We have yet to learn of all the books that were written by each of Arrius Piso's sons, grandsons and the rest of his descendants. And his descendants became the future emperors of the Roman Empire.

Arrius Piso's grandson Titus Antoninus became the Emperor Antoninus Pius. His successor, Marcus Aurelius was a great-grandson of Arrius Piso. However, Arrius' son Julius Piso, Julius' son and grandson were denied the throne, however, Julius Piso's descendants did eventually become emperors. But besides being emperors, the family members were the Popes of the church as well. After all, they were the ones who had invented the religion and built the churches. It only makes sense that they would be in control of Christianity and the Church. The 'Church' was a big money-maker, as there were many things associated with the church that generated a great amount of wealth. This will be further explained as you learn more about this subject.

As we dig more into this, you will see all of the important parts that Arrius Piso, his sons and grandsons played in making a new Roman Empire; of which they held complete and total control. It was from their position of money, luxury, power, and control that they produced and used all of the works that would seal their authority and completely fool the masses who were entirely clueless as to what was really happening. Had the masses known how they were being fooled and manipulated, they would have revolted and killed those who were oppressing them so harshly. We wish that more could be put into this one book, but that will have to wait until we can complete additional books to cover those areas.

We have to admit that it is amazing to realize just how far we have advanced in our research of this subject and the history of that time. It is so very complicated and must be researched on an extremely sophisticated level. So, read and enjoy learning about all of the things we have placed upon the pages of this very important book, that have never until now been brought to the attention of the general public in such specific detail.

ALIAS IDENTITIES IN ANCIENT HISTORY (How and Why they were Used)

HOW THEY DID IT: An example of how they did this was; that each family member would have a profile containing personal and identifying data. Each profile would contain information about their careers, who they were related to, when and where they were born, who were their immediate family members and their more distant ancient ancestors, etc. All of this was done for specific reasons and, was not kept under one identity, but several. In this way, they could say and write whatever they wished and no one would know who the writer or speaker really was, except members of the family.

At this point in time, it is uncertain as to whether or not the family formed a committee to decide the alias names for each member or just how much of what kind of data would be delivered (given out in public works) under each alias; or if the individuals in question were able to make those decisions themselves. We will share our preliminary opinions about this below.

Some things that tend to cause us to form the opinion that a committee was set up to decide these and other things are; a) This is something that they were very serious about doing, b) doing this by committee would assure that each individual would receive the credit (acclaim) due them as decided by the group rather than any individual, and c) this way would also help prevent arguments within the family (or the theory would suggest that at least), and d) we also know that more research is needed on this subject, and we are now attempting to have that completed at a later time. But, we can state factually that some of the aliases and their accompanying data appear to have been assigned or left to later generations to place into their own writings. And lastly, e) it would seem that a committee would be needed just for the purpose of avoiding confusion. Consider that they had to contend with securing the fame of recently deceased family members, and the current (contemporary) generations, and those yet to have their own careers.

One thing, among many others, that was needed would have to be how to decide just how far a person's identity should be hidden. Meaning, just how many aliases they would need in which to divide all of the data for each particular person. It is precisely because history was done (left to us) in this way, that Roman history NEVER gives all of the data out about any individual under their public identity. The information that will allow persons to find the true relationship of these persons to each other is given in ways that cannot be discovered or realized without first determining the alias names or alter names of any given person who would otherwise only be known to us under their public names.

WHY THEY DID IT: We realize that ancient history has been examined in a very limited way that does not allow one to venture beyond certain concepts, or as the phrase used these days, "think outside the box". In fact, the very thought of Roman authors having used pseudonyms or alias names is difficult to understand because of that limited mindset. Perhaps that is why, before now, this has not been explored in the way in which it should have been many years ago.. The authors did this, so as to give information about themselves and yet not arouse public suspicion over the fact that all of the persons who were writing history and becoming emperors were all related to each other. In this way, they could hide this fact and create the appearance that many diverse persons were writing, as this gave the false impression of an amount of 'freedom' existing in the Roman Empire (and thereby gave 'hope', although falsely, to the masses). And, further, they could also retain power for their own family without the populace ever learning that they were being tricked, lied to and used .

Time and time again, we encounter recorded instances of alias identities in different places for different things, within the lifetimes of those Roman aristocrats, authors and rulers. What this may mean is that not only were the writers fooling us, the readers; but they and others using aliases in their own day were actively deceiving whole towns, cities and provinces in their everyday lives! There are many examples that can be cited; one that comes immediately to mind is that of Arrius Piso. Abelard Reuchlin says of Piso in "The True Authorship of the New Testament," that; "Piso also shows his presence in these provinces (Pontus and Bithynia) - and also via Pliny's (Pliny the Younger) letters.

As Claudius Aristion (a form of Aristo/Arrius), he was the leading citizen of Ephesus (in Bithynia). That was the leading city of the province of Asia, located southwest of Bithynia. As Flavius Archippus the philosopher, Piso had been honored by Emperor Domitian; the emperor "commended" him to Pliny (Lappius Maximus, an alias used by Pliny) in Bithynia; and he ordered Pliny (Terentius Maximus, another alias of Pliny) to buy Flavius Archippus (Arrius Piso) a farm near Prusa. And the people of Prusa voted him as Archippus, a statue."

Now, if we had that statue of Flavius Archippus, aforementioned above, we would be able to see just what Arrius Piso looked like at that time! The ordinary people of that town did not know who they were really honoring!

Overlapping or transposing characters (lives): the best example of the writers pointing us toward the right direction in order to discover what was being done and discover who was whom regardless of the aliases that they were using is, that which we are given by "Plutarch" by his showing us how to "compare lives" with his work "Parallel Lives" (of the Noble Greeks and Romans), which consists of a listing and comparison of 46 famous ancient Greeks and Romans.

We have just answered why they had to use alias names, but why was it (as we found while doing this research) that they used so many different aliases? One reason that has already been stated was simply to make it appear to the public that many more persons were writing in their time than actually just a few. But, the necessary reason was because they could not give too much information out about each (to the public) as being any one "person"... or in any one place (book or literary work), as it would be too apparent just who they really were and what they were doing. They were doing something wrong, very wrong. They were deliberately deceiving the public and feeding them lies.

What we (the N.C.S.) are saying is, in other words, it was not in their best interest to make it 'easy' for others to find out what they were doing, as that would be defeating their purpose. The use of alias names was the solution to their problem of 'wanting' to tell who they were and what they had done, and at the same time being able to do that without jeopardizing the "institution" that they had in place. Their solution worked and allowed them the ability to say things about themselves and, promote ideas, etc., that under one identity would be too much to reveal to the public under their public identity. With aliases, they could say as much as they wanted and still preserve their family lineage and much more without anyone researching history ever knowing the truth, at least not until now.

As we learn more about the royal language and the various ways that they used language to both say and also to disguise what they were saying and actually meant, we found that they used every method that they could think of to make their system work. It is strange to think that in all of the studies made of the New Testament texts and of the history of that time that so many scholars have actually missed all of this for so long! It was always there and some scholars certainly could have found this if they had actually done the research. Why did they not put this information into the public arena? Why has this information been allowed to go unmentioned?

Why has it seemingly been covered up? Christianity would not continue to be a business today had this information been let out to the public. Somehow there seems to have been/be a driving force behind trying to prevent this information getting out to the public.

The royals made extensive use of two things in order to accomplish their goals; acrostics, and abbreviations. They used acrostics in a number of ways, but it appears that one of the most common ways was to use words that were spelled so as to have meaning within the letters that were used. These words, then became what we might call or include with others as 'key words'. This will be a subject matter for another time as we examine the usage of such words. Pertaining to the use of abbreviations, we can find the use of these in instances where a part of one name is combined with a part of another to produce a 'new' name or a nickname. As you go on to study this subject you will find examples of this being illustrated.

NOTES: See "The True Authorship of the New Testament," by Abelard Reuchlin, ©1986, Chapter titled "The Creation of the Church," pages 9-12. Perhaps during Arrius Piso's lifetime some average Roman citizens met and knew him as he had gained their confidence and made their acquaintance (using other identities). It may well have been that since he traveled extensively and often that he had different names that he used in different places. He states in his own works that the Jews (meaning the Pharisees) had many opportunities to kill him before he could make the new religion - and he taunts them about this. It seems that he was not content with deceiving people with only his literary works, but also in his real life as well.

A LIST OF ALIAS NAMES

This is a list of the various names used by members of the Roman royal elite. Many of these royals were closely related to the Flavians. Their primary or better known names or in some cases, their 'real' names are in upper case lettering. Please bear in mind that this is only a partial listing. But it should serve to aid the reader and researcher until a larger, more comprehensive list becomes available.

In no particular order...

1. AGRICOLA: Gnaeus Sextus Q. Petillius Cerialis Julius Agricola T. Aurelius Fulvus Rufus

2. TRAJAN: M. Hirrius Fronto Neratius Pansa Trajanus Ulpius Lupus Nerva Pudens Marcellus Julius

3. POMPEIA PLOTINA: Claudia Phoebe Hispulla Calpurnia Pisa Arria Fadilla Sacrata Domitia Lucilla I

4. DOMITIA LUCILLA II: Corelllia Hispulla Sabina Arria Lupula Julia Fadilla Arrionilla

5. CORELLIA MARCELLA: Eunice Statoria Rupilia Faustina

6. TACITUS: Cornelius/Cornutius Tullius Neratius Priscus Calestrius Tiro Palma L. Publius

7. CORELLIUS RUFUS: Q. (Quintus) Musonius Rufus T. Aurelius Fulvus

8. ARRIUS C. PISO: Flavius Josephus G. Caesoninus Junius Paetus Gallus Philo Antonius Primus, ect.

9. PLINY (THE YOUNGER): Gaius Plinius Secundus L. Appius Maximus Terentius Ignatius Nigrinus, ect.

10. BOIONIA PROCILLA: Servillia Procilla Prisca Lois Cleopatra Serrana/Serena Procla Quadatilla

11. FABIUS JUSTUS (C. PISO): Fabius/Flavius Justus Calpurnius Piso Justinus (the) Martyr Minicius M. Annius Verus

12. BAREA: Q. Marcius Barea Sura Soranus

13. JULIUS C. PISO: Severus/Servianus Ursus John/Jude/Hyrcanus

14. SUETONIUS: Titus Antonius Suetonius/Sertorius Irenaeus Tranquillus Aurelius Fulvus Boionius Arrius Antoninus Pius Augustus Tatian C. Ummidius Quadratus

15. PROCULUS C. PISO: Sillius Proculus Calpurnius Piso Tertius/ Agrippa/Simonides/Simon

16. SILANUS C. PISO: Caesennius Silvanius/Silanus Calpurnius Piso

17. JULIA SABINA: Flavia Julia Sabina (Titus' Daughter)

18. ARRIA (THE ELDER): Caecina Arria/Mary/Mariamne (The Elder)

19. LUCIUS C. PISO: P. Clodius Thrasea Paetus Lucius Calpurnius Piso L. Caesennius Paetus

20. ARRIA (THE YOUNGER): Flavia Sabina Atria Galla Caecina Arria (The Younger)

21. FANNIA: Flavia Arria/F. Annia Calpurnia Pisa/Piso

22. JULIANUS C. PISO: Julianus Calpurnius Piso M. Annius Verus Timothy Neratius Marcellus

23. FLAVIUS ARRIANUS: Flavius Arrianus/Appian Barnabas Marcus Cornelius Fronto Ptolemy

24. FLAVIUS SABINUS III: Titus Flavius Sabinus III

25. MARCUS AURELIUS: Annius Verus Antonius/Antoninus Germanicus Parthicus Sarmaticus Lucian

26. SENECA (THE YOUNGER): Gaius Lucius Annaeus Seneca (The Younger)

27. HADRIAN: Publius Hadranus/Adrianus

28. DOMITIA PAULINA I: Domitia Paulina (Pollina) I

29. DOMITIAN: Sextus Curvius Tullus Curtus/Curtius (Titus Sulla?)

30. DOMITIA LONGINA: Domitia Longina

31. NERVA: Marcus Cocceius Salvius Domitius Cornelius Fuscus Nerva

32. ALEXANDER C. PISO: Alexander Calpurnius Piso Andrew/ Andronicus

ARRIUS PISO AS EPICTETUS

Arrius Piso was 'Epictetus'. His discourses were recorded by his grandson Arrian (Flavius Arrianus). 'Epictetus' lived on into the reign of Hadrian (117-138). Which is true as Arrius Piso lived on to 119 C.E. We know this really was Arrius Piso because he was a crippled (lame) Greek 'slave' (like the characters of the NT refer to themselves as 'prisoners' and 'slaves' of God). He was a 'Greek' because of his ancestry, and as he wrote in Greek, and finally, had moved to Greece. During Nero's reign, he heard lectures of Musonius Rufus, before he was 'freed' (from Nero, that is). Musonius was expelled from Rome by Domitian (as was Arrius). Arrius settled (for a time) in Nicopolis, Epirus where he started a school. Arrian was one of his students. And why not? Arrian was his grandson!

JOSEPHUS (ARRIUS PISO) AS PHILO OF ALEXANDRIA

(1) As Josephus, Arrius Piso who has already been discovered to have used many, many alias identities had written some mention of Philo in his works – which should, raise some red flags. There are a number

of things to look for when trying to establish the true authorship of ancient texts, and the alias names and identities used by those authors. As for Arrius Piso also writing as Philo, the pieces of that puzzle fall into place when each are discovered and then reviewed together to reveal the full picture.

(2) We always keep our thoughts of motive in all actions and we keep our minds as agile as possible. So, we think why would Josephus (Arrius Piso) want to make mention of Philo? Could it be for the very same reason that he mentions 'Jesus'? That is, of course, to historicize him and make him appear to be a real person who authored the works attributed to him. Then we ask what purpose would he have for doing that? The answer is so that there would then be (or 'appear' to be) another 'Jew' writing public works in Greek! Without the works of Philo, Josephus, as a Jew writing in Greek, would stick out like a sore thumb! So, the purpose was to defuse any suspicion regarding Josephus as (supposedly) a 'Jew', who was writing in Greek! Which was, it appears, the only language in which Arrius Piso was actually proficient! He could write a bit in other languages, but Greek was his main language.

(3) Facts. During the process of researching other things regarding Josephus/Arrius Piso, facts in evidence were found that shows Arrius Piso did indeed also write as Philo. For one thing, Piso was 'Jesus', and 'Jesus' was (a) made to be god, and 'God' is presented as 'Love', and 'Philo' means 'Love'. Therefore, that all merges together as a proof. Furthermore, as if this string is not enough where we find Jesus as 'a god', we also recall the statement that Jesus was supposed to have made in the New Testament; "I and the Father (God) are one." So there again, we see Jesus as one and the same as 'God', and so on. Secondly, the only place ever found in the primary history sources that makes the claim that Philo was a real person by citing a pedigree, as far as we know, is the works under the name of Josephus! He makes Philo a descendant of King Herod – just as he, Arrius Piso, really was a descendent of King Herod.

(4) More facts. The 'Logos' of the New Testament is found in the works of Philo. A more detailed explanation will have to be offered about this elsewhere, but 'logos' is 'The Word' as the Gospel of John starts out by saying; "In the beginning, was the Word, and the Word was with God, and the Word was God." This, is another way of saying that 'God' had simply started out as an IDEA or concept that was written down

as a word. In other words, a literary creation. But again, as we have seen in the corresponding words and phrases that were found before, between the works under the name of Flavius Josephus and the New Testament, we see the same kind of evidence in the works of Philo. So, then we pursue the proof that these corresponding instances offer by the 'chances' of such similar things occurring between these different works. Another thing that comes to mind is that writing as Philo, Arrius Piso could use that as a 'hidden method' by which he could artificially pre-date certain things so as to create even more illusions and to solidify his claims made elsewhere in his other works. In effect, acting as his own witness! So, writing as Philo provided him the opportunity to mention in extra-biblical works (supposedly 'historical' works) what he was already doing with the New Testament texts – setting the scene/theme of the story in an earlier time!

Whereas the works that Arrius Piso wrote as Flavius Josephus were known to have been written circa 70-90 C.E., the works of Philo were backdated to circa 20-40 C.E. This brings to mind the line in Dio Chrysostom (21st Discourse, Vol. II, page 283); "… surely you have noticed what some of our booksellers do? Because they, knowing that old books are in demand since better written and on better paper, bury the worst specimens of our day in grain in order that they may take on the same color as the old ones, and after ruining the books in the bargain they sell them as (if they are) old…" So, we can envision how they accomplished the task of creating new 'old' authors and their works and introducing them into the marketplace and into 'history' so as to create whatever illusion that they desired or needed.

(5) Writing as Philo enabled Arrius Piso to write things that he could not write in other works or would not dare to, in any case. It is here, in the works of 'Philo', that he gives his view of the TWO races of men. This, in case you are not familiar with it, is where he alludes to there being only TWO races of men and those 'races' are found out by deduction to be (a) the royal race, and (b) the common people.

THE MENTION OF CHRIST IN FLAVIUS JOSEPHUS

(An Examination of Arrius Piso as Flavius Josephus)
What we are doing with this examination is to address a kind of mindset that we see out in academia today as well as in various groups of so-called (secular) scholars, and others who have it in mind to go the route

of uncertainty as making historical items 'appear' non-valid, rather than pinning them down with facts. Therefore, we are taking one of the best examples of this type of thought and exposing it for what it really is; a type of thought that was responsible for turning what was essentially a created original written idea into a rumor, which, in turn, has been accepted by many, erroneously, as a 'fact' of being an interpolation,. And that is the rumor that the mention of 'Christ' in the works of Josephus was spurious - a later addition (an interpolation), supposedly done by Christians. This is incorrect. It was in fact, original to the texts. We shall go on to prove this with our other studies in this area, which we will discuss here.

"Did Josephus Write it?" was originally information that was broadcast on the American Atheist Radio Series (program No. 356). And was first broadcast on August 23, 1975 according to the American Atheists magazine where it was published in an article of the same name, Feb. 1988 (pg. 39).

The subject of the article was the paragraph in the works of Flavius Josephus that mentions Jesus Christ. Madalyn O'Hair introduced and then apparently read a work that American Atheists had received from someone identified with the user-name of "Historicus". That article was titled "Did Josephus Write It?" ,and was supposedly originally written in 1972. This is the background on one of the main modern-day sources for the promotion of the idea that the mention of Jesus Christ in the works of Josephus was a later addition to those texts.

Here is our answer to that idea by answering this article point by point. Bear in mind that the reason for "Historicus" and all others who have tried to promote the idea that Josephus did not write the line about Jesus Christ in his works is simply to discredit the Christian claim that Jesus was historic and the authentic son of their God. Those who try to say that the "Testimonium Flavianum" appearing in (Josephus'/ Arrius Piso) work "Jewish Antiquities", where Josephus/Arrius Piso once again is trying to historicize Jesus as a real person is a later addition by Christians, were not aware of what they were doing. In trying to claim the "Testimonium Flavianum" they were really doing the opposite of what they had hoped to achieve. Below, you will find the actual text from the article as published in the American Atheists magazine in quotations, with Roman Piso's comments to that text immediately below each quotation. And that is the form that our answer to this article will take here. [Note that there was an article written by Roman Piso, 1998 titled "About Josephus' Mention of

Jesus" that had already addressed and answered this very same idea. And now, the article with our (the N.C.S.) reply to it...]

Historicus' writing is shown as (Historicus); Our response is shown as (NCS):

(Historicus) "Christianity, without Christ, cannot be. It is just that simple. Because of this, a veritable duel to the death has existed between Atheists and Christians for as long as the Atheist has been permitted to duel. In early Christian history, he was simply murdered for heretical beliefs. Since 1667, he has been permitted to speak with only the harassment of prison terms, loss of employment, and complete boycott by the Christian-dominated culture, with severe economic and psychological sanctions against him."

(NCS) The beginning of the above statement shows the true reason for "Historicus" and other atheists to try and promote the idea that Josephus did not originally mention Jesus Christ in his works. "Historicus" and other atheists did not understand that they did not need to 'bend' the truth nor fear it, as the truth will bear out that despite the fact that Josephus/ Arrius Piso did indeed originally mention (Jesus) Christ, that did not at all mean that Jesus Christ was not actually fictional - or that this could not be proven.

This idea turned into rumor, which had become as accepted 'fact' to some, is really a desperate attempt to make it appear that there isn't any validity to the mention of Christ in the works under the name of Flavius Josephus - which is very short-sighted and is not to the credit of genuine scholars. As a matter of fact, this idea does more to keep people from finding the actual truth regarding the mention of Christ in Josephus' work than anything else. This is so because on the surface, it appears to answer the question of why the mention of Christ appears there. But in reality, it does not answer that question. And that is because it is only speculation without any basis in fact, whereas our (the N.C.S.) explanation fits the rest of the facts involved.

(Historicus) "The argument always reaches to the historical writers of the time of Jesus Christ. Of course, the Christian historians will not admit that god certainly could have preserved the records of his only son, had there really been a god. In the United States, we did a much better job preserving the documents which made us a nation than did god to preserve the documents which would have proven the authenticity of his son."

(NCS) Yes, the argument always reaches to the historical writers of about the time in which the New Testament story was set, and that Jesus

Christ was supposed to have lived. In reality, they were made to appear to have been written several years after the supposed time of Christ. That is because any true scholar or researcher knows to consult the earliest texts available in order to find the truth. Anything written later is not as reliable as those which were written closest to the time in question.

(Madalyn) "The Atheist historians are not all that brave as yet. One of ours, indeed, refuses to even identify himself. He writes under the name of Historicus."

(NCS) I wonder if we will ever learn who this person really was. He had a bright idea, but he was not a real historian as he failed to realize that it is only the truth that will ever solve this, not what one wants the case to be. Little did he realize what he did would color the view and understanding of so many for so long a time, keeping them from even questioning things which they should have questioned.

(Historicus) "Despite the fact that the basis of anti-Semitism in the Western culture is Christianity, when it comes to the all-important argument of whether or not a Christ did exist, the average Christian theologian calls upon evidence of the despised Jew -- particularly that of Josephus, a Jewish historian who lived about the time that Christ's life should have been reported and who was of major significance in the Roman culture. Josephus lived from A.D. 37 to 100 and he was the official (or one of the official) historians of the Roman Empire. Therefore, he had access to documents and information which others might not have had."

(NCS) Yes, it is true that anti-Semitism the world over arose out of Christianity. The statement that 'the average Christian theologian' relies upon evidence from Josephus speaks volumes as to why this "Historicus" was trying to take that evidence from the theologians. But in his haste, he makes waste. It will be shown just why this "Historicus" was really not a true historian, but rather someone who wanted to promote a certain view for specific reasons - the specific reasons that we are now discussing. At the point in time when "Historicus" wrote this, there wasn't any information yet available to the public regarding the truth about Flavius Josephus, namely that this was a penname of Arrius Calpurnius Piso - a Roman who was a "Jew" due to his descent on his mother's side. He was a Jew by birth, not by belief. He was not descended from Jewish "believers" or followers, but from Jewish leaders of the Sadducean sect. Professional scholars and researchers do not use "A.D." They use "C.E." instead, which stands for "Current Era," or "B.C.E." for "Before Current Era, not B.C".

Well, Historicus writes about this important problem, the historicity of Jesus Christ, quite often. Here is one of his later works, written in 1972, which is permitted to be reproduced in whole or in part. Let's see what he has to say about this question in an article titled "Did Josephus Write It"?

The article continues…(Historicus) "Scholars have often averred that the Jesus of the New Testament is a myth, that he never had existed, and that there is no historical evidence to substantiate the claims for his existence advanced by the Christian church. At first the religious apologists scoffed at this contention and attributed the statements of the scholars to pure wickedness, seeing in it but another attempt of Satan to lure more souls to Hell -- this, and nothing more."

(NCS) A "myth" is one thing, a deliberately created composite character designed to deceive is another thing. The idea of myth gives the appearance of something that is generally viewed as benign. What we are dealing with here is a character that was deliberately fabricated out of many different sources for the specific purpose of being representative of a new "religious" ideology that would encapsulate and protect old political ideologies. Namely, that of the nationally institutionalized practice of slavery, so that slavery would appear to be something that was 'normal' and just a natural part of life. Those persons who invented Christianity were descendants of those same people who invented Judaism and so, they felt that they had the right to either make a new religion and destroy the old, or remake the old one so as to be entirely different. The religion itself, to them, was merely a 'vehicle' by which they could achieve various goals which they had set forth. To those who were the 'believers', it was what they were deceived into thinking it was - and they could neither see nor understand anything different while they believed in the lie. Both the God and the Devil (or Satan) in the story were created by the same persons.

Anyone who understands ancient dramas should be able to realize that in order for a "God" or character who is playing the 'good' personification in a story, would naturally also require the opposite of that character, the bad, in order to play off of it in comparison. The essence is the conflict. One or more characters have to portray 'good' while another or others portray the opposite. The New Testament, and the Gospels in particular, are written as a play would have been written. There is a narrative, there are acts and scenes. This is not how an account would be written about something that really happened. "Hell", too, was a created concept that pre-existed even the Jewish religion. In the Jewish religion, "Heaven" (or the idea of it) is introduced as paradise in the form of "The Garden of Eden" (as Heaven on earth). But this too, also existed as an idea prior to the making of the Jewish religion.

These are ideologies that were synthesized by royals for use in "managing" control over the masses whom they ruled. All of this is the way of ancient times when kings and other forms of rulership over the masses was all there was, basically dictatorship by the royals. It does not belong to a time when people have freedom of speech and are able to democratically vote for and elect those whom are their political representatives.

(Historicus) continues: "But as the study of mythology advanced, historical parallels were constructed and the truth began to dawn upon unprejudiced persons. The similarities proved to be extremely destructive to the accepted beliefs about the life of Jesus."

"Dupuis, Strauss, Drews, Smith, Roberson, and others brought together sufficient evidence to establish upon a firm foundation that there is nothing in all history to prove that the Jesus of the New Testament ever walked the face of the earth."

"Contemporary writers displayed an amazing lack of information about Jesus. Here was a man who performed miracles that astounded the multitudes, yet his acts are not found recorded in the books of historians who noted occurrences of much less importance. Remsburg, in 'The Christ', names forty-two writers who lived and wrote during the time or within a century after the period when Jesus is said to have existed, and from all their writings only four passages are to be found that might possibly support the historicity of Jesus. And of these four passages, not a single one can stand a critical test."

(NCS) The article by Historicus does not mention the names of the four ancient writers who wrote a mention of Jesus or Christ. These were (in chronological order): 1. Flavius Josephus/Arrius Piso. 2. Pliny the Younger. 3. Tacitus. 4. Suetonius.

(Historicus) "It is agreed that the strongest of them is the passage found in the works of a Jewish historian, Flavius Josephus (living between the years A.D. 37 and 100). Professor Arthur Drews, in 'Witnesses to the Historicity of Jesus', states that "he [Josephus] is the first profane writer who can seriously be quoted for the historicity of Jesus."

(NCS) It might be noted that Flavius Josephus/Arrius Piso did not live in the time in which Jesus was supposed to have lived (the time in which the New Testament story was set) - yet the way in which he writes about him in that passage is as if he knows who Jesus is/was. It is written "matter-of-factly." It gives the reader the impression that he intends to write more about "Jesus," and if not in the work he was currently writing, then "elsewhere." In other words, in the Gospels, as the main character.

(Historicus) "If the passage in Josephus is genuine, then strong and in fact formidable proof is offered for the Christian claim along historical lines. On the other hand, should this passage be found a mere forgery, a clumsy interpolation, then the strongest element of proof for the historicity of Jesus in the whole mass of ancient literature crumbles and dissolves."

(NCS) That is only so if you do not consider that the ancient writers themselves were in fact deliberately deceiving the reader in all instances, not just in texts that were supposed to be of a religious nature, but those that were supposed to be 'historical' as well. The contention of those who are working on this new view of ancient history explain in the following manner. 1) that many unfounded assumptions have been made by those who have put forth the view that all ancient writers are to be believed in a wholesale fashion as if they were all indeed just who they claimed to be and 2) as if they did not have any ulterior motives for making the statements that they did; that they were not deliberately misleading and deceiving the reader.

And that is what we have found to be wrong. Ancient writers were not only deliberately misleading the reader, they were in fact all closely related to each other and were indeed 'royals' writing for the purpose of "crowd control," if you will. There was not any freedom of speech , as only royals were allowed to write and only royals had the means to produce written works. The idea that anyone could and did write in those times was a facade that was created by royals long before they invented Christianity. As stated, it was a facade. One that served a deliberate purpose. And that was to give the masses the impression that if they wanted to "speak" out to others about their concerns that they could if they really so desired. The truth was that they could not do so at all. So, in viewing the writings under the name of Flavius Josephus or of any other ancient author, we must re-think this in entirely different terms. This new view of ancient history is finally what explains this subject fully and in even the finest detail. We must not be afraid to pursue this new line of reasoning to its fullest conclusion.

(Historicus) "Josephus was the author of 'A Defense of the Jewish Religion'. In this he showed himself to be a fervent believer in Judaism -- a point that must be kept in mind in view of the passage attributed to him depicting Jesus as the long-awaited Messiah. At the time he wrote, the

Christians constituted a very small sect, of no particular political or social importance. Late in the first century, Josephus completed his classical work, 'The Antiquities of the Jews'. In this book is found a complete history of his race, dating from the very earliest age, according to the knowledge of his day."

"While in the midst of the story of a Jewish uprising, the narrator in this book is interrupted by the following irrelevant passage: "Now there was about this time Jesus, a wise man -- if it be lawful to call him a man, for he was a doer of wonderful works and a teacher of such men as receive the truth with pleasure. He drew over to him both many of the Jews and many of the Gentiles. He was the Christ. Although Pilate, at the complaint of the leaders of our people, condemned him to die on the cross, his earlier followers were faithful to him. For he appeared to them alive again on the third day, as god-sent prophets had foretold this and a thousand other wonderful things of him. The tribe of Christians, which is called after him, survives until the present day" [Jewish Antiquities xvii, 3, 3]."

"Would Josephus, who wrote with such careful sequence, break the unity of his narrative to observe, with Christian piety, that "about this time [lived] Jesus, a wise man -- if it be lawful to call him a man, ... he was a doer of wonderful works... He was the Christ... he appeared to them alive again on the third day, as god-sent prophets had foretold," etc? All this we are asked to accept as coming from Josephus, an extremely pious Jew!"

(NCS) Actually, Historicus is trying to make a deduction based upon what he knows. However, he is operating on a different level than we are. Again, as previously stated, he assumes too many things. And that is his failing in terms of understanding this subject correctly, and in what he was able to subsequently deduce as a result. Oh, and Josephus/Arrius Piso did not write in "careful sequence" always as Historicus claims. There are many instances where he breaks off into other time periods and subjects while he is writing. Instances of this kind can be provided easily by anyone who is expert in the writings of Josephus.

And, in case anyone missed this, "Josephus" was a penname of a Roman by the name of Arrius Calpurnius Piso. He was a "Jew" only in the sense that he was descended from Jewish leadership on his mother's side. He was privy, because of this, to ancient Jewish history and was also helped by his Herodian cousins with whatever else he needed to know. He was especially friendly with his cousin Agrippa II. He, Josephus/Arrius Piso was not "pious" in the least. He may have "pretended" to be pious as

Josephus, but that is not the same as actually being "pious." Examples to prove this will be supplied in upcoming books on the subject.

(Historicus) "We should be inclined to think that this Jewish historian, after noting a matter of such prime importance in the history of his people as the coming of the Messiah, would proceed to elaborate on it, to impress its significance upon his religious brethren, for the Jews at that time were bestowing great attention on matters pertaining to the coming of Jesus the Messiah. In fact, they were awaiting the Messiah with painful impatience and desperate hope."

(NCS) No, not so. Again, this is an illusion, a 'facade' that was created to go along with the general impression that the writers were trying to make regarding this subject - as they did not want what this was truly all about to be found out or discovered by the public at large for as long as possible. In actuality, the books that we know of as the "Old Testament" were re-written later in the form of the Greek Septuagint so as to match what was stated about Jesus in the New Testament. The New Testament was finished by about the year 140 CE, while the books of the Jewish religion which is called the "Old Testament" were not finished being re-written until about the year 180 CE.

The impression which had fooled Historicus is that he thought that the Jewish zealots and rebels were so implying because of their zeal for their religion and the assumption that he makes is that they were because they were awaiting their Messiah. The reality is that the leaders of the Jews (the Pharisees) were actually engaged in a war with the Romans over the issue of slavery. But since the official authors of history at the time were the Romans, they of course could not state the truth of what they were really doing. The best that they could do was to 'allude' to what the truth was and give instances that may be cited to support that truth when/if anyone could deduce it correctly.

(Historicus) "But Josephus, as soon as he is through with the Jesus passage, the heaven-sent Messiah, the long-awaited Christ who was to bring peace and happiness to all those suffering under the cruel Roman heel, goes on, as though nothing of unusual importance had been touched upon, to make the statement: "Also about this time another misfortune befell the Jews;" and the text continues leisurely with the story of how Tiberius expelled the Jews from Rome. Attention is immediately arrested by the wording, "another misfortune befell the Jews." What 'other' misfortune? If Josephus had written the joyful Jesus passage, would he have continued with "another misfortune" and then told of Tiberius and his expulsion of the Jews?"

(NCS) The answer is "YES!" The reason Historicus does not understand why Josephus/Arrius Piso has said things as he has is because he does not understand who Josephus really was or what he was actually referring to. He is 'secretly' saying that the character Jesus (his invention) was a great misfortune to the Jews, and this is because he, Josephus considered "Jesus" to be a great weapon against the Jews. This is evidenced by how, as Jesus, he Josephus/Arrius Piso could aim Christian believers in a direction of hatred toward the Jews who were at war with Rome. The Gospels and the New Testament as a whole, was written as a parody of a part of that war as satire. And this too, will be illustrated in great detail by those who know the real way in which these things actually transpired. Many instances of anti-Semitism have already been found and defined within the New Testament. Now you know the real reason why those passages are there.

(Historicus) "About this passage affirming Jesus as the Christ, a number of observations might be made. Josephus is obviously ignorant of the occurrences connected with Jesus and his followers. As one who accepted Jesus as the Messiah who the "god-sent prophets had foretold," Josephus must certainly have gathered zealously all available information about him. Yet, the conscientious narrator of Jewish history fails utterly to note such exciting events as: (1) the triumphal entry of Jesus into Jerusalem, (2) his acclaimation (being 'acclaimed') as the Messiah, (3) the riot before the governor's house, (4) the surrendering by the Sanhedrim of one of their people to the Roman authorities, (5) the disappearance of the body from the grave. It is not an easy matter, as Professor Drews states, to show that these events were too insignificant for Josephus to record. The Acts of the Apostles (2:41) shows the new religious sect (Christian) entering into deadly rivalry with the old religion. It is difficult to understand how Josephus, a thorough historian in his way, could have failed to include the aforementioned events in his work had these incidents occurred during the life of Jesus."

(NCS) As has been stated many times, "Jesus" was a composite character - not a real person and not merely a 'myth' either. The reason that Josephus had made what mention he did of "Jesus" is because he was historicizing him so that there would be a reference to him as appearing to have been real, even though he was not and never had been. Josephus (aka Arrius Piso) did not need to mention all of the things that the Gospels said about Jesus as that was not the purpose of what he did. His purpose was served by the mere mention of (Jesus as) the Christ. As a matter of fact, even without mentioning the name of the Christ in his works, he (Josehpus aka Arrius Piso) identifies the Christ that he is speaking of as 'Jesus' by making mention of James, his brother. In addition to this, there are numerous other NT elements included within his works. One in particular, is John the Baptist.

(Historicus) "That he noticed messianic disturbances in the times is amply proven in his 'Antiquities' (pages xviii, 4, 1). Here are noted the false Messiah and his attempts to induce the Sameritans to rise against their Roman masters. Then there is the incident of Judas, the Gaulonite, who created a disturbance of the people against the census of Quirinus; the story of the pretending prophet, Theudas, who claimed to possess the power to divide the waters of the Jordan to allow his followers to cross in safety."

(NCS) Historicus does not realize at all as to what any of what he has stated about each of these pertains. His view is seen as totally uninformed from our perspective. What is glaring here is that he has again assumed far too much. Notice that Historicus is under the impression that each of these things was about the Jews awaiting a Messiah, and in his rather simple reasoning he has drawn wrong conclusions as he is obviously unfamiliar with the subject of the Jews at that time. The thing that really distorts his view of the Jews is that he is unable to define just who the Jews were at any given time or place that is being spoken of and so, without any other options, he lumps them altogether and things about them in extremely simple terms. Historicus, for example, does not recognize Judas, the Gaulonite, as "Judas of Gallilee" a great Jewish hero in the war. Nor does he recognize Theudas as also being a great Jewish hero in that war. In fact, because of his outlandish ignorance of the Jews he fails to recognize that the Jews are in fact belittled and ridiculed by Josephus/Arrius Piso. And this is because, as we have said, he (Josephus) was really a Roman merely pretending to be a Jewish historian.

(Historicus) "In 'Witness to the Historicity of Jesus', Professor Drews says (page f) "Does anyone seriously believe, in fact, that Josephus could have concealed from the Romans, who had long ruled over Palestine and were accurately informed as to the disposition of their subjects, the messianic expectations and agitations of his compatriots and represented them as harmless, in works which were especially concerned with their" strained relations to their oppressors?"

(NCS) This is not what was really happening at the time. This is what the writers wanted readers to think was going on. There were not any messianic expectations or agitations by the Jews, this is only what the Romans wanted people to think so that they would not realize what it was really all about. The only real "Jews" who actually mattered were the leaders, and the leaders were very wise people. And as for the Jews who were fighting the Romans against slavery, the Pharisees were the Jews who were of particular concern to the Romans.

It should also be noted that as the leaders of the Jews were all descended from the same family as those who were their opposition, they were also aware of the fact that their religion was false and was only a 'method' used to inspire their people to achieve their goals. They were not irrational religious people as portrayed in works under the name of Josephus. Josephus/Arrius Piso in fact, was actively trying to promote superstition and belief in the paranormal and this is done for psychological reasons - the purpose was to make 'fertile ground' for belief in the new religion (Christianity) which he was, at the time, making.

(Historicus) "The most important and illuminating fact, however, is that the passage about Jesus as the Messiah is not to be found in the early copies of Josephus. Not until the 'Ecclesiastical History of Eusebius' (about A.D. 300) do we come across it, and it is claimed that all reference to this passage is worthless as historical material because of the deliberate falsifications of Eusebius."

(NCS) Though Eusebius was indeed a greatly deceptive figure (actually this was a penname of Constantine's half-brother Julius Constantius), there was not any reason for that to have been a passage that was added later. As one may now fully understand, there was not any reason for that passage to have been mentioned before that time as it was already readily available right there in the works of Josephus. In fact, if the passage had been mentioned, it might draw unwanted suspicion that might point towards Josephus as the inventor of Jesus - and they most certainly did not want to do that. After a reasonable amount of time had passed, and the New Testament texts were translated Greek into Latin at about that time (circa 300 or so CE), it was then relatively 'safe' for Eusebius to make mention of that passage without fear of anyone finding it as a source for raising questions about Josephus/Arrius Piso as the inventor of Jesus.

(Historicus) "Jakob Burkhardt considers the wily Eusebius to be "the first thoroughly dishonest historian of antiquity." He elaborates on his character as follows: "After many falsifications, suppressions, and fictions which have been proved in his work, he has no right to be put forward as a decisive authority; and to these faults we must add a consciously perverse manner of expression, deliberate bombast, and many equivocations, so that the reader stumbles upon trapdoors and pitfalls in the most important passages. ('Leben Konstantins, Second edition, 1860, pages 307, 335, 347)"

(NCS) The first thing to state and point out once more is that, all ancient writers were writing in this manner. All who wrote were royals. Not any of the 'average' persons were ever allowed to write books in ancient times. The royals all wrote in a misleading and deceptive manner. And, this does include the Jews of the time as they in fact were not as 'free' as we may think at first, to do what they pleased. They were watched closely by the Romans in all that they did and all that they wrote. They (the Jews) were allowed to write in ways similar to the way that the Romans did, but anything beyond that would have meant the possibility that they could have been wiped out forever as a people. And when they considered their options they knew that it was far more important for them to continue to exist than not to; as they were the only ones who were in the unique position of supplying information about the subject of the war and the truth about the invention of Jesus and Christianity, that the Romans did not want revealed.

(Historicus) "Also of the utmost significance is the absence of the Josephian passage in the controversies of the early church fathers. Not only is the passage not to be found cited in their voluminous disputes, but one fails to come across even a mention of it in works where it would undoubtedly have appeared had it been in existence at that early day. It is not in the polemics of Tertullian, Cyprian, Justin or Origen. Valuable indeed would this passage have been to Justin in his dialogue with Trypho the Jew."

(NCS) As was already stated, all of these writers were of the same family; they were royals. They well knew not to do anything to point to Josephus as the inventor of Jesus - and that included bringing up the mention of Jesus in the works of Josephus. If they ever needed to cite that to anyone in person, they could easily do that using the actual works of Josephus. And so, there was not any need for them to cite that passage in their own works.

(Historicus) "Chrysostom, a careful reader of Josephus, wrote in the latter part of the fourth century. The quotation of the Josephian passage would have weighed strongly in favor of the church. But no mention is made of it in his works, and we are inclined to accept the view of Remsburg that he was "too honest or too wise to use it." "

(NCS) No, the true reason has already been stated; Chrysostom was an alias of Arrius Piso aka Flavius Josephus.

(Historicus) "Canon Farrar, in his 'Life of Christ' (Volume 1, page 63), sums up the case in the following words: "The single passage in which he [Josephus] alludes to him [Christ] is interpolated, if not wholly spurious." " "The verdict of history has thrown this passage out. And thus the church remains without one iota of tangible evidence to uphold its claims for the historicity of Jesus."

"And thus speaks Historicus" [Madalyn O'Hare ends]

(NCS) History has not thrown the passage out. Only people who are uninformed of the true nature of this subject have disregarded it, as they do not understand that Josephus was not really who he appeared to be and that his reason for putting that passage into his works was to historicize "Jesus" because Josephus/Arrius Piso is the one who invented him! Jesus was not a real person. He was a fictional character that was written into a fabricated story line, and "played" by Arrius Piso (aka Josephus) as the story went along. The Romans needed people to 'believe' that Jesus was real, and that was the purpose of writing him ever so subtly into 'history'.

That people have mistakenly reached the wrong conclusions about this subject was inevitable. But wrong conclusions do not have to continue. What most people read is a translation that is more of an interpretation into English from the Greek of the works of Flavius Josephus. They generally do not know how to read it in the Greek for themselves. Therefore, they cannot rightly judge the passage accurately. Many of these people are not even familiar with the works under the name of Flavius Josephus to any real extent; and yet, they quickly offer their opinions as if they are qualified to do so. It is natural that people want to give their opinions, whether they are experts on the subject or not. But by giving opinions that are far from correct, they create (or perpetuate) the illusion that something is right, correct or true, even if it actually is not. This appears to be the case here. So many people have offered their unqualified opinion that other uninformed people tend to think that so many people cannot be wrong. As we now know, many people have been wrong about many things, for a very long time.

Secondly, asking if the passage in Josephus mentioning Christ is a later addition, is basically the wrong question to ask in order to get the correct answer. Sometimes, many questions have to be asked so that one question may be answered. This means that sometimes asking one question is not enough. The question here should be, "Did Josephus invent Jesus (Christ) and author some of the New Testament?" That way, you start to find the other instances in the works of Flavius Josephus which correspond to the New Testament. When you discover the rest of the connections between the works of Flavius Josephus and the NT, the mention of Christ is then understood as the paramount purpose of those works. In other words, the primary reason for Josephus (Arrius Piso) writing his works was in order to historicize his invented character - Jesus (as the 'Christ').

This was his "honor" and privilege, and his alone. Why would he not take it? Not to, was not the nature of those particular persons. Again, the real reason for Josephus writing his works was to include some mention of his invention (Jesus) so as to make him appear to be a real person in 'history'. Why would he write over 115 items that we can find in the New Testament and not include the main star of the show? He wouldn't miss out on that opportunity - and he didn't. The mention of Christ in the works of Josephus are original to those texts, and for ulterior motives! Thirdly, there are certain words and phrases used in conjunction with literary devices which we find in the works of Flavius Josephus (Arrius Piso) that we find also used in the New Testament texts. Those are things which will be discussed later in other works of the New Classical Scholarship (N.C.S.).

ARRIUS PISO AS T. CLAUDIUS ARISTION AND TITIUS ARISTO

In the Index of the works of Pliny the Younger we find (Ti) Claudius Aristion, leading citizen of Ephesus (and president of the Provincial Council of Asia), cleared of a charge heard at Centum Cellae, VI. 31.3. As we compile our data we learn of more and more of his (Arrius Piso's) aliases, and gain more information about his life, which helps us in our quest to find more of his alias identities.

Also in the index of Pliny: Titius Aristo, the Jurist, often cited in the 'Digest', he was a pupil of Cassius Longinus, and a member of Trajan's consilium with Neratius Priscus: he survived a serious illness, I. 22; letters justifying Pliny's light verse, V. 3; and asking for advice (from Pliny?) on legal procedure, VIII, 14.

With this information, we continue to follow the 'trail' which the writers of the time had created. We have already found out, writing as Josephus, Arrius Piso claimed that Vespasian had bestowed upon him the name 'Flavius'. But he was already a grandson of Vespasian's brother

(T. Flavius Sabinus). Moreover, it was not only the 'Flavius' name that he had inherited and used, but also Titus and Sabinus. He also used the 'Vespasian' name as well; in a round-about way.

Further, Arrius Piso used the inherited name of his ancestor Aristobulus (note 'Aristo' in the name), in Romans 16:10. Here, he is called 'Aristobulus', but this also honors the name of his Herodian ancestor Aristobulus, son of king Herod 'The Great'. We found 'Aristarchus' (Arrius) mentioned with 'Secundus' (Pliny the Younger) in Acts 20:4. These two, Arrius Piso and Pliny the Younger were the original "Dynamic Duel." We then realize that 'Aristarchus' is really a combination of 'Aristo' and 'Archippus'. See Acts 19:29; 20:4; 27:2. Col. 4:10 and Phm. 24. From here, we looked back to the works of Pliny the Younger and found Arrius Piso there as 'Flavius Archippus', the philosopher.

ARRIUS PISO AS MATURUS ARRIANUS

In the index of Pliny the Younger, we found Arrius Piso as 'Maturus Arrianus', a Roman knight of Altinum, his letters with speech in Attic (Greek) style are discussed. Arrius Piso is 'Maturus Arrianus' because he was 'Apion' (which is also Arian/Arrian in Royal Language), and because he is the older Arrian; as he has a grandson named Arrian. Arrius Piso, wrote in Greek, and Arrius Piso was at one point, a Roman Knight. When these writers stated that someone was 'of' (or from) a certain place, this is not really saying what it appears to mean. The assumption is made that when such things are said, it means that someone has been born and raised at the place mentioned. But, what it really refers to in many cases, is just where the person owned a villa and property.

ARRIUS PISO AS THE SUPREME AUTHORITY

As 'Antonius Primus', Arrius Piso was called 'the supreme authority' by Tacitus. Arrius Piso was head member of the Supreme Court in Athens, Greece. A reference made to this is found in the New Testament (Titus 3:16); "To Titus, chosen first (Primus) overseer of the assembly of (the) Cretans." Note Arrius Piso as 'Titus'. When Arrius Piso went to live at Crete, he became a "Cretan." And, as written in the NT, we see "Cretans are always liars." Which was actually a line taken from Epicurus. As Dionysis, the Areopagite (see the mention of 'Mars Hill' aka 'Arius Pagos'), Arrius Piso was a member of the Supreme Court of Athens (Acts 17:34). As Titius/Titus (Claudius) Aristo, he was a Jurist. (T.) Claudius Aristo, remember this is in Pliny, as is Titius Aristo (the Jurist). Galatians 2:3; "But not even Titus, who with me, being a Greek, was compelled to be circumcised..." II Cor. 2:13; "... at my not finding Titus, my brother..." Note that this was Pliny writing, II Cor. 7:6; "But he who encourages those brought low encouraged us by the coming of Titus..." I Cor. 6:12; "All things to me are lawful..." (Meaning that he, the author, Paul (Pliny writing) can get away with anything, that he was above the law) "... I will not be brought under the power of any."

ARRIUS PISO AS MONTANUS

This is such a very interesting area of our study of Arrius Piso and his many alter-identities. Firstly, the name 'Montanus' does not appear to be a name which was made-up or invented by Arrius Piso (although, more research does need to be done regarding this). It seems to be a name inherited from his ancestors. This is because we found that people from an earlier time had this name, and as they were in written ancient history, they most certainly had to be royal - and thus, a common ancestry from the earlier point in time on up to the later time of Arrius Piso is highly probable. Under the supervision of other royals, in order to inherit the name and use it, a valid link back to someone with that name had to be established. We will, of course, have to give a very close examination (at some point) of all of those with the name 'Montanus'.

'Montanus' "is spared out of consideration for (the death of) his father" when Thrasea Paetus is put to death under Nero (Ref. Tacitus, Annals, XVI. 33). Also in Tacitus, we find that there is a 'Curtius Montanus' who was living while Nero was emperor. This Curtius Montanus is described as a habitual composer of "abominable verses." That is, "bawdy literary material." Sounds a lot like Arrius Piso, doesn't it? Ref. Tacitus, Annals, XII. XVI.

As Flavius Josephus, Arrius Piso had an ancestor named 'Matthias Curtus' (or 'Curt(i)us'). Ref. Flavius Josephus, Vita, 1.1 (Whiston Translation). This shows the inheritance and use of the name 'Curtus' and then we notice it being disguised simply by adding an 'i' to it. We see this very same device used over and over again along with several others, in an attempt to decieve the reader.

In our research we found that there is a 'Julius Montanus' in Tactius (he is a senator), who is said to have encountered 'the prince of darkness'. This is during Nero's rule. One might well think that Tacitus is calling Nero 'the prince of darkness'. This Julius Montanus was forced to destroy himself (just as Gaius Piso was) by 'the prince of darkness'. Now, this would make some sense when one thinks of Nero's opponents (such as Gaius Piso and Arrius Piso) as those "of the light." Furthermore, we think of Arrius Piso (Gaius Piso's son) as 'Jesus', because as Jesus he was the 'prince' who was also "the light of the world," i.e. 'the prince of light' (as opposed to the 'prince of darkness'). Therefore, this Julius Montanus appears to be Arrius Piso's father, Gaius Piso. Ref. Tacitus, Annals, IX, XIII.

In time, there will be much more written about Arrius Piso as 'Montanus'. There is just much more about this man than can be covered here. Many of the other things pertaining to this subject are either a) extremely complicated, b) requires a great deal of background knowledge, c) involve cross-references which will need to be provided and explained, or d) all of the above.

As we have seen, there appears to have been a very subtle allusion made to Arrius Piso (as 'Jesus') with the title 'prince'. This was done by inference for those who were already privy to all of this background knowledge. Does this make sense? It does if it fits the rest of the facts involved. This recalls Pliny calling Trajan 'prince' (or rather Arrius Piso as co-ruler with Trajan, being addressed or referred to as 'Trajan'. The two were sharing the same name), in his Panegyricus. There is much more about Arrius Piso as 'prince', but perhaps that may fit better in a book about the royal language.

Pliny (the Younger) has a lot to say to help us "connect the dots" between Arrius Piso and his alias names. Another reason why 'Montanus' is an appropriate name for Arrius Piso is because when Domitian had exiled him (or 'stationed' him) in Bithynia, he went to live near Prusa. Where near Prusa? Mount Olympus.

Pliny said to 'Trajan' (that is, Arrius Piso being addressed as 'Trajan'): "Prusa, at the foot of Mount Olympus, in Mysia." He said this because it is true that geographically Mt. Olympus is technically in Mysia (see the boundary line on maps given of that time), but on the other side of Mt. Olympus is the town of Prusa, which is a part of Bithynia (see the Index in Pliny, Book II, of II). Also, Prusa is the birth place of Dio Cocceianus Chrysostomus (Dio Chrysostom). But Dio Chrysostom was not a real person, he was just a penname created by Arrius Piso. This means that the alias name "Dio Chrysostom" was created in Prusa, by Arrius Piso, while he was living there.

And, as we have also found, 'mountain' is how the family referred to Arrius Piso. (because he had lived on Mt. Olympus), and 'island' is how they referred to Pliny the Younger. And this is because of Pliny having been sent to an island; and because this is reflected in the New Testament texts in his character 'Paul'. As 'Paul', he is shipwrecked on an island. Given our knowledge of this, we find this in Rev. 6:14; "every mountain and island were moved (i.e., 'moving')..." This is alluding to Arrius Piso as 'Montanus' and to Pliny as 'island'. And why should they 'move'? Because these were only their nicknames, they were really living people, who could move!, just like any other real person. There are places in the New Testament that refer to "talking to 'a' mountain." Well, it is not a real mountain which is being spoken to, but a real person who could talk (Arrius Piso). This is how they hinted and alluded to the truth of the matter. Ref. Mark 11:23; Matt. 21:21; Luke 23:30.

Another thing to note is that there appears to be a parallel between Curiatus Maternus and Marcus Aper with Curtius Montanus and (Marcus?) Domitian Aper in Tacitus (in his 'Dialogues'). In addition to these things, there is a play on words going on which involves various spellings of similar words. For instance, the Greek word 'oros' is 'mount' or mountain (as found in Mark 10:1). There are many hints at the relationship of this word with similar sounding or similarly spelled words, particularly in the form of inside jokes and puns. Rev. 1:3 is very instructive on a scholarly level. Translated it says, "for, the time is near." The word 'time' here is spelled 'kaipos' (in Greek). The author obviously had in mind that the reader would realize that the word for 'time' could also be spelled 'ora'. If one thinks of the two words mentioned here as names, they would be the same excepting that one is in the masculine form while the other is in the feminine form. This means that the word "time" is synonymous with "mount" (mountain). But this also extends to include the word for "hour" and even "season" in Greek. Jesus is thought of as being associated with a fish (in this case, with the word 'nun'). And this is how, in Matt. 14:15, we find "... the time is now." The 'time' (aka, the 'mountain') is (also the word) 'now', because the word for 'now' could be spelled 'nun' (i.e., 'fish'). And thus, as a 'fish', Arrius Piso as Jesus can make a joke out of saying, "eat of my body and remember me!"

And as we see Pliny the Younger "praying" to Capitoline Jupiter, we realize that Arrius Piso has the alias name "Capito," and that his ancestors had the name "Linus"; and also that Arrius Piso was descended from the person who had been known to royals as 'Jupiter'. And that by living on Mount Olympus, he was in effect, the new 'Jupiter' (or Zeus) incarnate.

So, yes, Arrius Piso was then called "Capitoline Jupiter." This also explains other things that we will be discussing in future books on this subject.

Notes:

A 'Montanus' is mentioned in Juvenal, IV; 107, 131 (Loeb). Also see Pliny's Index for 'Montanus'. There is also a map in the Loeb edition of Pliny the Younger which shows Prusa and Mount Olympus. And see Ptolemy's 'Geography', Book V, Chap. I, for the town called Prusa (in Bithynia), near the foot of Mt. Olympus. Note that 'Ptolemy' was an alias name of Arrius Piso's grandson Flavius Arrianus (Arrian).

'Montanus' is found in Sir Ronald Syme's article titled 'People in Pliny', which was published in JRS (The Journal of Roman Studies), 1968-69, pg. 149-150. And in Tacitus, Hist., III, 35.2; and Tacitus, Annals, Book XVI, XXIX, pg. 381; and also Tacitus, Annals, Book XVI, XXXIII, pg. 387.

As we have also observed (but which bears mentioning again), these ancient authors resorted to the use of abbreviations to help disguise what they were really saying and meant. If you are still not convinced that "Montanus" meant "mountain" (and in turn, Arrius Piso) – the word for "(the) mountain" in Latin is "montem." If we see it abbreviated as "mont" and add the rest of the name "Montanus" then we have "mont-an(i)us." That is, rather, "mont-Annius." And we know that the "Annii" part of "Annii Verii" is really a variant form of the spelling of "Arrius" (with the 'r's and the 'n's interchanged, as was done by the use of the royal language). The result is "mont" (mountain), "Arrius." Thus, "Arrius, the Mountain." Ref. Tacitus, Hist., Book II, LXXIII, pg. 284-287, Loeb Classical Library edition.

ARRIUS PISO AS PLUTARCH

Previously the person calling himself Plutarch was thought to have been the Roman Emperor Trajan. However, comparing notes with those of Abelard Reuchlin, it is now thought that Reuchlin's information appeared to make a stronger case towards Arrius Piso writing as Plutarch. And so, this is what had been accepted. However, since that time, it has been learned that the reason Abelard had reached that conclusion is because Arrius Piso was in fact co-ruling with the Emperor Trajan and was also being referred to as 'Trajan' - and thus the confusion. But at the same time we arrived at virtually the same conclusion, without first realizing that fact.

When one thinks of the authors of the period in which the New Testament was written, Plutarch is often forgotten or ignored. As a matter of fact, there are other authors' 'works' of that time which are often not read, cited or even mentioned at all. Some of those do not directly pertain (at least on the surface) to history in the broader sense and, why this may be is understood. However, knowing that these authors often hid information in places where people were not likely to look; suddenly, these other works become important. Some works being referred to include that of; Frontinus, Martial, Juvenal, Lucan, Petronius, Arrian, Appian, etc. Taking a look at the works of Plutarch, we found such statements as: "Galba was somehow related to Livia, the wife of Augustus Caesar…" The author knew exactly how Galba was related to Livia, but that information was put out without explaining the relation in order to 'cloak' it so that it would not be obvious and therefore, would be left unknown by the general populace.

Also, in Plutarch, we found that Verginius Rufus played a large part in how things had progressed during the time of Nero and Galba – and that he was even a potential contender for the imperial throne. Yes, and it seems that what we should do is to make a list of those who almost became Emperors, so as to help us all understand just how these people were related to those who did become Emperors, and to each other as well. There are many, many things that need to be done to help get a clearer picture of all of this. Lists, lists and more lists need to be made. The chore gets almost out of hand when one figures in the fact that all of these must then be cross-referenced so as to be prepared as needed in order to use them effectively.

There are some interesting things found in Plutarch's account of those times, but one usually will not be able to see all of those unless they are using the Loeb Classical Library Edition and can read Greek! Some translators had taken it upon themselves to delete some words and names which appear in the original texts. One such instance is the name given for Titus Vinius. There is the name 'Polla' which is not shown in the translations, and there is the spelling of 'Vinius' which is really "(A) ouvinius" [Afininus]. This, taken together renders the name as 'Titus Aufinius/Au(l)finius Polla/Pollo'. It appears that the word/name 'polla' was mistaken by the translators to mean something other than a part of the name, which, seems to have been the intent of the author. It could even be seen as a disguised masculine variant as 'Pollatonus' by combining 'Polla' and 'ton' (the Greek words, which were deleted by translators).

In our reading of the history of those times, we found that Otho was once a close friend to Nero. One in which Nero had trusted. But a time came when Otho and Nero were at odds with each other because of their mutual affection for Poppaea. In Plutarch it is stated; "Otho, accordingly, came into peril of his life; and it was strange that although his own wife and sister were put to death by Nero on account of his marriage with Poppaea, Otho himself was spared." Another person who played an important role in those times was one Dolabella. This name should be kept in mind and examined at every opportunity. There are many more things in Plutarch's works which need to be addressed and explained. . For now, we will try to examine what we presently have before us.

There are important statements such as: "And quickly there came also friendly letters from Mucianus and Vespasian, who were at the head of large forces, the one in Syria, the other in Judaea." It has also been mentioned that Mucianus was 'close to becoming Emperor'. Abelard Reuchlin has identified Mucianus, as an uncle of Arrius Piso. Apparently Mucianus was a brother of Arrius Piso's mother.

And here is another statement that calls out for an explanation; "And this is the account given by Secundus the Rhetorician, who was Otho's secretary." Who was Secundus the Rhetorician? One would think this to have been Pliny the Elder. And, in Plutarch's works, we found a statement made by Otho to his young nephew 'Cocceius'. This Cocceius became Emperor Trajan. He says; "And now, my boy, this is my last charge to thee; do not altogether forget, and do not too well remember, that thou hadst a Caesar for an uncle."

Plutarch's Lives (see 'Galba and Otho' in the Loeb Classical Library Edition), contains a general index which is extremely helpful to the researcher.

SO, ARRIUS PISO NEVER EXISTED?! So saith those who are with the church and others who support the church, or those who just do not know, or those who have another agenda they want to promote.

Regarding comments and claims, that he never existed, by those who would make such a claim just because Arrius Piso was not mentioned in history by his full true name, we must say this;

(1) Although, it may well be that he was not mentioned in history under his full true name, but even that has not been proven to be true - that is only how it 'appears' to be at the present time. There may be instances or at least one instance where he actually was put into history under his full true name, and we just have not found it for whatever reason. One possible reason may be that they did this not by use of 'common language', but instead by the use of the 'royal language'. Which, we will be discussing later.

It is possible that he was mentioned in a part of either Tacitus' or Suetonius' works that did not survive in the existing copies that we have today; or, that may have existed in any number of other works of that day. Perhaps even the book or books that gave his full true name were systematically 'recalled' (or destroyed) by his descendants over the course of many years for fear of those even existing. So definite conclusions regarding this in the negative sense (stating that he did not exist) just cannot be made because of this and other factors still to be discussed. The facts must be examined, and when they are, they show that he did exist and that his name was "Arrius Calpurnius Piso," and that he created the fictional character 'Jesus'.

(2) If there was never an Arrius Piso, then how is it that he had sons and a long line of descendants? How is it that with history actually happening in a very controlled way that persons in later history which was being controlled by that very family still appear with the "Piso" family name or trace their descent from him?

There was a later claimant to the Roman throne who had the name of Piso and he claimed to be a descendant of those Pisos who had conspired against Nero; which, was Arrius Piso's family! How does one explain the carefully preserved Piso family genealogies with ingeniously hidden links to their other relatives? With the various reconstructed genealogies we know just which persons were really related to other persons of that family and we can trace those back to the same common ancestors to find out real (true) names and decipher those from alias names which were also used. No one is saying that this is or was an easy task to do. Persons must have a vast knowledge of this research and all other related studies, such as the work done by the Piso Project, the New Classical Scholarship, and also knowing about the Royal Language and the Royal Supremacy concept in order to do this and to verify these reconstructed family relations.

Aside from that, we will now be able to slowly test the genetics of those family members whose bodies have been found and those which will be found in the future to confirm the family tree information! One thing that could be done fairly easily (as long as the real bodies have not been switched), is to test the bodies of certain Popes to see if and how they were related to each other and if they are found to be related when 'history' tells us that they were. We will then have proof of deliberate deception committed by Piso family descendants who were and, those who became leaders of the very religion which they created!

Obviously, the earlier the genetic material samples the better for our purposes. But that is also the most difficult to find. The bodies of nine Popes (that we presently know of) were placed in the catacombs at San Calixtoin Italy, and the bones of these Popes were apparently removed (by the Vatican?). Some very small samples of DNA evidence may still remain in these tombs. If so, and if there is enough, then genetic testing will be able to show that all of these Popes were closely related to each other. And again, that would prove our point. Genetic testing need not be limited to Popes, but may be applied to any and all of those whom we find to be involved and/or related or descended from the original Piso family.

There are many more sources of DNA evidence to prove our genealogies, therefore, the truth about history. All of the writers of history, all of the "saints" and other figures known to us from ancient history up to about the 1500's should be found to have ties to this family. It is only a matter of time before a group or groups start exploring the DNA evidence to either prove or disprove relationships as we have detailed them. We are quite confident of our findings, so we say; "let's do it"!!!

(3) Not all archaeological evidence is in on this either. Even if Arrius Piso was never mentioned in history by his full true name as he certainly had reasons for hiding his true name. There could also be evidence found about him and his true name in other forms such as tablets made of various materials which might have survived, or in other forms that may yet be found that would contain that full name. But, when one realizes, because of all of the evidence that there is already showing that history had to have happened only in one way and, that way was that the history of that time and on this subject presented, was written by one family and in a very tightly controlled fashion, then light falls on another realization.

That is because only these persons were writing all history, this made it possible for them to do certain things and get away with doing them, which would not have been possible otherwise. Namely, being able to refer to each other by first names only, or by alias names which they knew and understood, or even simply by inferences. That Arrius Piso's full true name is not in the history that we know of and are familiar with presently, is really only a minor point in the greater scheme of things. Also, it may well be that the leaders of the Jews who were at war with Arrius Piso and his family, may have left a scroll or scrolls with his name on them; scrolls that have never been translated and made available to scholars or the general public as yet - or which simply have not yet been found.

Moreover, that piece of physical evidence could already have been found. If that is so, it may still exist somewhere. Perhaps being in the possession of a private citizen or in the hands of some very powerful person. Or, it may have been found and destroyed. Again, because of what the Piso Theory research means, it is not necessary for Arrius Piso's true full name to have been given in history. It would be, however, another great support for the truth and evidence already found. Therefore, the blanket statement "Arrius Piso never existed" is really quite ridiculous at best.

(4) Even though at this point in time we do not find Arrius Piso's full and true name in history in any outright fashion, it does, never the-less exist in forms that intentionally invite reconstruction via deduction, each example, of which is supported by related evidence. To give exact examples here and to explain them would be too lengthy, but those are shown and explained elsewhere. Besides the actual names that include some form of the name "Arrius" or "Piso", there are many examples of deliberate hints, clues and inferences directed towards the discovery of his name as "Arrius Piso." These too, are examined and explained elsewhere.

Remember to note that Arrius Piso's name could have been spelled out in full by a means in which would not be "obvious" to readers. For example, Roman histories and other texts that were written in Greek would follow a different syntax and the words ran together. This would allow a person writing in that language to run two or more words together to render a word or name that would not easily be seen by a reader - even in that language! So, imagine how we could easily miss many such things by reading translations instead of the oldest versions known in that original language. It is entirely possible that a version of the name "Arrius Piso" may be found 'hidden' in this fashion within some old text by using this method. That is to say, Arrius Piso may well eventually be found in ancient history or some other ancient text and it may be very plainly spelled out; but just not in an obvious way.

(5) This is information or knowledge that was shared by royals in general in those times. This means there were other witnesses to what was actually transpiring and who was around at the time. Just as there is reconstructive evidence in Roman history, there is likewise that which is found in the Jewish texts that have survived. The Jews themselves had to be very subtle in what they wrote about this subject as it was a matter of survival for them. They were the closest witnesses to this and they were well aware of the persons involved, and they left us confirming evidence as well. Do not discount the Jewish proof texts!

Note: At the time of this writing we have found that there is at least one source in ancient history where the name 'Arrius Calpurnius Piso' was preserved. And that is found in the Talmud. Abelard Reuchlin discovered this and so he is entitled to write about his discovery first.

In the end, there is much more evidence to support this writing and research and, detailed facts about Arrius Calpurnius Piso than there is about the claim made by believers and the church that "Jesus" was a real person. It is the "type" of evidence that differs. And that is to be expected pertaining to the invention of the fictional character 'Jesus' for the reasons that we specify. That is, any additional evidence in support of our findings which we have pointed out, would have to be exactly the kind that we found! And not as blatant outright admissions by Arrius Piso or another member of the family.

A BRIEF EXAMINATION OF 'THE HISTORIES' OF CORNELIUS TACITUS

Let's now touch upon some of what is found in the 'Histories' of Tacitus. 'Cornelius Tacitus' was a penname of the person known as 'Neratius Priscus'.

1-With bits and pieces here and there, Tacitus tells us valuable information about the war that was raging while Christianity was being constructed. He, along with other writers of his time, supply us with information about just who was on which side of the war. In observation of the whole war, in order to designate individuals in their respective positions during that war, the same terms are being used here, that were used in WWII for those who were of the 'Axis' with Germany, and those who were of the 'Allies' with Britain and the United States against Germany. And so, those who were with the Pisos will be called those of the 'Axis', while those who were allied with the Pharisees will be designated as 'Allies'.

2-For your edification, before we proceed in this examination of the 'Histories' of Tacitus, a list of some of the Roman Emperors and on which side they were on in the war of the Pisos against the Pharisees; Nero was an Ally, Galba and Licinianus Frugi Piso were of the Axis, Otho is a bit of an enigma in this respect as there is much confusing information. What is suspected is that Otho was really out for himself, although there was at least the pretense of being an 'Ally'; but when considering that Vitellius could not stand for Otho to be Emperor, it appears that Otho was actually on the side of the Axis.

3-And Vitellius was an Ally of the Pharisees as he actually did some things to show himself to be such; for example, he was a champion of the slaves and common people by rallying them together to fight the adversity to their freedom. Vitellius was also killed by Arrius Piso (in history, under the name of Antonius Primus). Knowing just who was an 'Ally' and who was a member of the 'Axis' is key to understanding why it is that they did certain things during their lives and/or rule. As one will observe, the particular role of each of these in their position as either an 'Ally' or in being of the 'Axis' is consistent throughout – and because this is so, it serves as a proof that this is indeed true.

4-"The armies in Germany were vexed and angry, a condition most dangerous when large forces are involved. They were moved by pride in their recent victory and also be fear, because they had favored the losing side. They had been slow to abandon Nero; and Verginius (Rufus), their commander, had not pronounced for Galba immediately; men were inclined to think that he (Verginius Rufus) would not be unwilling to be emperor himself; and it was believed that the soldiers offered him the imperial power." This is important to know, as this allows us the knowledge that this person, Verginius Rufus was a person who might have become emperor of Rome.

5-"The East was as yet undisturbed. Syria and its four legions were held by Licinius Mucianus (Lucius Piso), a man notorious in prosperity and adversity alike. When a young man he had cultivated friendships with the nobility for his own ends; later, when his wealth was exhausted, his position insecure, and he also suspected that Claudius was angry with him, he withdrew to retirement in Asia and was as near to exile then as afterwards he was to the throne." This appears to be an indication that Licinius Mucianus was also close to have becoming emperor! Tactius goes on to say about him; "... he was a man who found it easier to bestow the imperial power than to hold it himself."

6-In the footnotes of the Loeb Classical Library edition of Tacitus' 'Histories', there is this commentary; "Licinianus Mucianus had been consul under Nero, and in 67 (C.E.) was appointed governor of Syria. After Vespasian claimed the imperial power Mucianus became his strongest supporter..."

7-Now we read; "Neither Vespasian's desires nor sentiments were opposed to Galba, for he sent his son, Titus, to pay his respects and to show his allegiance to him, as we shall tell at the proper time."

8-Exactly. This is because both Galba and Vespasian, along with Vespasian's son Titus, were of the 'Axis'. This should be enough information for now on this subject as this is a lot to think about and to consider, as well as to try to confirm for yourself by your own research. And because we now have started the use of the designators 'Axis' and 'Allies' in terms of Roman history with regards to the war between the Roman and the leaders of the Jews, we will now find it much easier to identify each individual in their respective role as either one of these. To make this simpler and easier, we might well think of the 'Allies' as the good guys, while the 'Axis' would represent the bad guys.

TACITUS AS NERATIUS PRISCUS

In order to discover the alias names or alternate names that were used by the Roman figures who hitherto have only been known to us by their public names, one must search out all possible leads, leaving no stone unturned. Let's begin this with info from "The True Authorship of the New Testament," by Abelard Reuchlin. In it, Reuchlin states; "The family also put their friends into the New Testament story. Justus (Piso) inserted Cornelius Tacitus, the Roman historian. He became Cornelius, the Roman centurion in Acts, Chapter 10, who was devout and feared God; and he was also (Cornutus) Tertullus, the prosecuting attorney against Paul in Acts 24:1-2. Tacitus reciprocated by dedicating his 'Dialogues on Oratory' shortly after the year 100 to "dear Fabius Justus"." This, on page 14 of Reuchlin's booklet.

Reuchlin further states (on pg. 17); "Now the family had other writers place Jesus and Christianity in prior history. First, the Pisos used their friend Cornelius Palma, the jurist. Writing under the name Cornelius Tacitus between 115 and 120, he mentioned Christ and said that he had founded the Christians and had been crucified by Pontius Pilate; and also detailed that Nero had caused Christians to be torn by dogs and burned on crosses." (Ref. Tacitus, Annals, XV.44, Loeb Classical Library edition) Reuchlin also claims to have found Cornelius Tacitus as "Cornutus Tertullus" and "Cornelius Palma, the jurist." It is also Reuchlin who is credited (by us here) for discovering Tacitus' other identity as "Neratius Priscus."

Now as for Cornelius Tacitus as Neratius Priscus, it may well have been that the late Roman history scholar Ronald Syme knew of this and several other items relating to the truth about ancient Roman history. Syme is a major source for the critical examination of these names and personages, because of his extensive work in this area (See his articles in JRS - The Journal for Roman Studies, a periodical which may be found in many college or university libraries). Syme says in his article "Tacitus: Some Sources of his Information",* that; "The case of the jurist Neratius Priscus is instructive, consul suffect in 97, the same year as Cornelius Tacitus." And this is precisely how one needs to work through these names and identities - carefully following EVERY clue.

One finds Cornelius Tacitus as Cornelius Palma, a jurist. And we see Neratius Priscus (also a jurist), as consul suffect in 97, the same year as Cornelius Tacitus! Persons who research these names need to consult lists of consuls (as well as other lists of compiled data), compare dates and events, titles and positions, names of relatives and even cross-reference material. There most certainly are other names in Roman history of that time or near it that contain the names "Cornelius" and "Priscus", but one must work through these names with caution. It is like following bread crumbs, a "trail" that was deliberately made to be like a great maze at the same time! It indeed, is like a tangled web! Which brings up another point. Those who have fancied themselves 'experts' in ancient history and who have been used to thinking of Roman names in terms of first and last names will realize that thinking in that way is like putting on a blindfold. You will never discover the truth by limiting your thinking in that way. As we are proving here, 'history' was not done in that way. It is a much more challenging (sophisticated) thing that most people have yet begun to imagine. Facades of that type were created deliberately to keep you from easily discovering the truth.

In Syme's article titled "People in Pliny,"** he says; "Proconsuls of Asia and of Africa are likewise not much in evidence. Asia from 103/4 to 120/1 (the list is now complete) exhibits only two, viz. Cornelius Tacitus and Cornelius Priscus." So, here we see Tacitus again with the same title, in the same place, at the same time... this time with another "Priscus" (who just so happens to have the name "Cornelius" as well). As a person works through the maze of names in this way, the evidence mounts and the likelihood of coincidence disappears. By the way, we also again see "Cornutus Tertullus" in association with "Cornelius Tacitus" and "Cornelius Priscus" in the footnote regarding these two in the same article. More information should be gained from further examination of this, including the list of proconsuls of Asia and Africa of that time. It is by following such clues that we are able to finally piece together the truth in ancient history and find out who was really whom.

Moreover, in the same article, we find our friend Neratius Priscus (now known to us as the person who wrote 'history' as "Tacitus"), as the husband of Corellia Hispulla (See pg. 147). In addition to such overwhelming evidence as that which we find in following these clues, we continue to find (and disclose) even more.

When one reads, for instance, "The Life of Hadrian," by Aelius Spartianus, one learns that (at least supposedly); "There was, to be sure, a widely prevailing belief that Trajan, with the approval of many of his friends, had planned to appoint as his successor not Hadrian but Neratius Priscus, even to the extent of once saying to Priscus: "I entrust the provinces to your care in case anything happens to me." One would wonder just how it is that Trajan had thought to make Neratius Priscus (Tacitus) his successor. Well, having looked into this further by comparing the alias names of the emperor Nerva and those of Neratius Priscus, as well as doing more studies into the various alias names used by other persons of the time the reality of the matter has now come to light. "Neratius Priscus" is now seen as "Ner(va) Atius Priscus." Now, if this does not warrant more attention being given to this issue - what would?

Notes and references: Ref. Tacitus, "Diologue on Oratory", Vol. 1, page 231, Loeb Classical Library edition.

* Ronald Syme, JRS (Journal for Roman Studies, a periodical), "Tacitus: Some Sources of his Information," 1982, pg. 68. ** Ronald Syme, JRS, "People in Pliny," 1968-69, pg. 141. (And pg. 147).

"The Life of Hadrian," Aelius Spartianus, Loeb Classical Library edition. RE: Tacitus as "Cornelius Palma"; as Palma he was governor of Syria in 107, succeeded as governor of Syria by Fabius Justus (Justus Piso) in 108 CE. Also as Palma, he is cos. II (consul for the second time), in 109.

A merging of aliases: We find a mixing of the aliases of Tacitus, blending two, to make even another alias "Cornelius" of Cornelius Palma and "Priscus" of Neratius Priscus, to make "Cornelius Priscus". Using this identity, he reports the death of Martial to Pliny the Younger. See the works of Pliny the Younger in the Loeb Classical Library edition.

For more information on specifics you will want to get a copy of the booklet titled 'The True Authorship of the New Testament', by Abelard Reuchlin. You can send for a copy of this for about $8.00; send at time of request, from: The Abelard Reuchlin Foundation, P.O. Box 5652, Kent, WA 98064. Also be advised that the price of this barely covers the cost of printing and postage. And because of the fact that many libraries are run by Christians and those who are adverse to anything that contradicts their own personal beliefs, this booklet may not be found in many libraries at this point in time. This is strong information and there certainly are many people who wish to keep this information away from the general public and from scholars as well.

THE CONNECTION TO SENECA

Though it is true that recently we have not focused enough attention upon Seneca in his involvement in the synthesis of the Christian religion (in the studies of the Piso Project and in the other books of the N.C.S. thus far), we most certainly should and will. This is for several good reasons. When Bruno Bauer wrote his work "Christ and the Caesars," he made the observation that several areas of the Christian religion arose out of the ideology contained within the works of Seneca. Remember, the time when Bruno Bauer was writing this, was then 1877.

Abelard Reuchlin's work too, shows Seneca as an early and major player in the invention of Christianity. In Reuchlin's work "The True Authorship of the New Testament," he says that Seneca & Lucius Piso were working together* on a prototype containing the basis of Christianity (he says it was 'Ur Marcus', the prototype for the Gospel of Mark). However, more accurately, they were probably re-writing or editing a pre-existing prototype in order to perfect it – with the original having been penned by Arrius Piso's grandfather or great-grandfather who wrote Roman history as (Vellius) Paterculus, according to Reuchlin.

Abelard Reuchlin says that the 'Lucilius' whom Seneca corresponded with while writing his works was Lucius Piso as the name 'Lucilius' was a pseudonym or alias name of Lucius Piso. Besides this, we find Arria the Younger as a relative of Seneca via her maternal ancestry. Close family ties can be both supporting evidence and/or in some cases substantiating evidence by demonstrating and explaining motives. There are several indications (evidence) pointing to Vellius Paterculus as an ancestor of Arrius Piso, including certain places in the Talmud which Reuchlin plans upon exposing in his upcoming work on the subject.

One has to wonder when they read the phrase in 'The Revelation', "Here is wisdom…" (Rev. 13:18). Because wisdom is what Seneca is always talking about as if he was the source of all of it. And, it is true that when a person does examine the works of Seneca, they then do find (through critical and objective examination) the major basis and component material for the foundation of the Christian religion contained therein. Was the author of 'The Revelation' pointing us towards the works of Seneca?

Seneca makes the case for the placation of slaves, and tells how to do it. He discusses the subject of slavery and slaves throughout his 'Epistulae Morales'. But the strange thing is that he is not at all against slavery, yet, he talks about people who are poor (the common person) as if this were a virtue and even acts as if he is trying to get wealthy people to give up their wealth and study philosophy to become philosophers!

But his 'advice' does not make sense because he never takes a stance on slavery, other than to just accept it as a part of life. And he advises wealthy people to give up their wealth, while at the same time expecting them to keep their slaves! And he, himself, has slaves and is wealthy! So, given this, we find that his writings are really just propaganda.

Having read the works of Seneca and having also read what Bruno Bauer wrote regarding Seneca, it can be easily understood why it is that Bruno Bauer had reached the conclusions that he had about the works of Seneca. If one understands the researching of history as having to be conducted as a detective would perform his work, then the evidence begins to come forth to be understood for what it is. Seneca's epistles read like a primer for Christianity!

It is impossible to read Seneca's epistles objectively and not see his work as a supporting basis for many of the main (fundamental) tenets or elements of Christianity. For one thing, Seneca uses Romanized versions of elements relating to both the Jewish and Christian religions, alluding to them and mentioning them in his literary work. And, in the works of Seneca one also finds even more evidence that the original idea for Christianity was 'Catholic'. He talks about "holy water," and as other Roman authors do, he also alludes to the necessity of the 'confessional'.

It is almost ridiculous to try to point out all that Seneca says that relates to Christianity without him ever mentioning it by name. His work is thick with pro-Christian sentiments and ideas. He talks endlessly about 'God' and he uses words/terms that are key to the Christian religion. He puts forth ideas and concepts that are essential to the Christian religion and urges people to have 'philosophy' as a basis by which to live.

But what most people do not realize is that in the time in which Seneca was writing, 'philosophy' did not mean philosophy as we think of it today. Philosophy at that time meant anything that a person followed or believed in; meaning that by saying 'philosophy' he also meant 'religion'! And in the language that he used in his works (as if he were a Priest), he most certainly was aiming people towards belief in Christianity! He talks about a variety of things throughout his epistles showing the work to be one of specific purpose, and that is to put forth and strengthen certain ideologies. He writes in a way to bolster the morale of the soldiers in the military, for instance. While it appears that all that he writes has some certain purpose to it as propaganda rather than of real (genuine) personal opinion and commentary. He uses phrases such as "…equipped only with the courage of a soldier,…" (Seneca IV, 'Epistulae Morales' Book I of III, Epistle XXIV, Loeb Classical Library Edition). There are, by the way, ten volumes of Seneca's works in the Loeb Classical Library, three of which are his 'Epistulae Morales'.

He speaks about the need for slaves to be placated (contented) and calls attention to the great need for this particularly in his own time by making statements such as, "… just as many have been killed by angry slaves as by angry kings." He goes on to say how slaves of old used to be willing to give up their lives for their masters and, that this was because they were given an amount of respect within the household and how that had changed over the years. He says that slaves do not start as enemies of their masters, that masters cause them to become their enemies. He is definitely pro-slavery. This, at a time (as we now know) when there was an all-out war (the Romans in Judaea) raging on this very issue. So, this now can be demonstrated as one of the main reasons for the construction of the Christian religion; the placation of slaves and the preservation of the institution of slavery within the Roman empire.

Perhaps one day, time permitting, we should go through Bruno Bauer's "Christ and the Caesars" and make a commentary upon all of the instances therein where he charges Seneca with some involvement in the invention of Christianity. His work is rather massive and this would be a great undertaking, but it is something that really ought to performed to finally validate his great contribution to the study of the true beginnings of Christianity and the truth in ancient history. He (Seneca) talks about 'hope' and 'fear', and so, most certainly knew how to use those as components to get people to become trapped in belief. He puts forth not only the idea of 'souls', but also of the need to 'save' (preserve) them. He chastises himself, much the same way that Arrius Piso did while writing as Josephus, saying, "It is ignoble to say one thing and mean another; and how much more ignoble to write one thing and mean another!" But that is exactly what they were doing!

He also makes (disclaimers) statements to the same effect that Pliny the Elder did, in saying that "men are (indeed) mad," meaning 'insane'. That, seems to be the justification for what they were saying and doing. He makes the statement that, "only young minds are molded." Meaning that they need to be raised in the 'faith'; that religion should be a family tradition and children should be brought up in it (molded/indoctrinated) so that this will be their 'philosophy' for life. (Actually, religions today are doing this very thing with young children.) And, one can readily see Seneca's work as the source for several of the statements that are found in the New Testament. Some examples of these are: He alludes to the concept of 'original sin' and talks about sin throughout his works as well. He puts forth the idea of prayer as well, making it seem as if everyone is doing it and that prayers are answered! He is busily painting and making a picture that he hopes will cause people to accept and by which they will live and use in their daily lives! His writings are very nearly pure propaganda!

Some of the statements that he makes are; "the soul alone renders us noble." And, "we tie knots and bind up words in double meanings, and then try to untie them." Also, "...take heed, lest things, as well as words, deceive us." He also talks about a 'personal god' as opposed to the old concept of 'public gods'. And so, this shows why their invented 'Christ' was made to be such a 'personal god'. Seneca says, "God is near you, he is with you, he is within you." And he talks of a 'holy spirit', and we are well familiar with that term in the New Testament. Here is the encapsulation of the statement within the New Testament where it is said that mere mortals cannot understand the ways of God. He says (in an apparent quote), "A god doth dwell, but what god know(s), we (may) not." And he says directly, "for no one has knowledge of God." He also (as do other ancient authors), supplies us with the fact that these ancient royal writers already knew that the world was round. They make this point very clear in many ways, including their writings and even on their coins. Seneca says, for example, "Why do you wonder that 'globe-trotting' does not help you..." Notice the phrase "globe-trotting." Or traveling around 'the globe'. Well, this information should suffice for now.

SUETONIUS: A GRANDSON OF ARRIUS CALPURNIUS PISO

(The following reference notes are keyed to the Penguin Classics version of "The Twelve Caesars" unless otherwise stated)

In "The Twelve Caesars," Suetonius (aka Antoninus Pius) brings up the subject of cipher or ways of concealing what is actually written by saying how Julius Caesar kept personal notes and confidential messages from being read by others by putting them down in a secret code. (Ref. Suet., Julius Caesar, pg. 34-35, verse 56).

Suetonius cleverly hints at the "beast" in The Revelation as a horse (i.e. 'ippos' or 'Piso'!), when he is speaking of a charger (horse) belonging to Julius Caesar, he says; "This Charger (horse) of his, an extraordinary animal with feet that look almost human – each of its hoofs was cloven in five parts, resembling human toes – had been foaled on his private estate. When the soothsayers pronounced that its master would one day rule the world, Caesar carefully reared, and was the first to ride the beast..." (Ref. Suet., Julius Caesar, pg. 36, verse 61). Also note that he says that "the beast" (horse/ippos/Piso) had toes like a human! He was referring to a person.

Source for Rumplestillskin? I wonder if something stated by Suetonius did not form the basis for the story of Rumplestillskin. He talks about Augustus Caesar buying (at auction) his adopted sons (Gaius & Lucius), at a sham sale by touching (or tapping on) the scales 3 times with a bronze coin (which is gold colored). And then he goes on to talk about Augustus' daughter (and grand-daughters) being taught to spin (on a spinning wheel) and weave (weaving straw?), and how the girl/girls were severely restricted from doing anything that might be seen in the least bit as non-decent. (Ref. Suet., Augustus, pg. 85, verse 64).

Suetonius mentions "professional storytellers." (Ref. Suet., Augustus, pg. 92, verse 74). And Suetonius lets us know of the use of metaphors by royals when he makes mention of Augustus' favorite metaphor for swift and sudden actions; "Quicker than boiled asparagus." (Ref. Suet., Augustus, pg. 97, verse 87). There seems to be another underlying (humorous?) meaning to this statement. Could it be that this is a 'phallic' joke? He hints at another part of the Royal Language as being "phonetic spelling," and about Augustus using cipher (as he had also said that Julius Caesar did), and gives an example of what Augustus used in his cipher. (Ref. Suet., Augustus, pg. 98, verse 88).

He says that Augustus called for a group of friends and asked, "Have I played my part in the farce of life creditable enough" (Ref. Suet., pg. 105-106, verse 99). He jokingly wanted to say; "I swear by the Truth of God" (which is a joke), but instead makes it as Augustus having said; "I swear by the Gods of Truth." (Ref. Suet., Augustus, pg. 121, verse 21).

He talks about the real mindset of most of the royals by saying, "Tiberius did so many other wicked deeds under the pretext (pretense) of reforming public morals – but in reality to gratify his lust for seeing people suffer. (Ref. Suet., Tiberius, pg. 138, verse 59).

Suetonius talks about inherited name/titles by saying that such names (names/titles) were "adopted." He says, "He (Caligula), adopted a variety of titles (name/titles): such as "Pius," "Son of the Camp," "Father of the Army," and "Caesar, Greatest, and Best of Men." (Ref. Suet., Caligula, pg. 159, verse 22). He talks about the use of "double-entendre." (Ref. Suet., Caligula, pg. 163, verse 27). It is also worth noting that it is Suetonius who is the first to mention the name "Columbus" in a public work, saying; "... a gladiator of this sort, called Columbus, won a fight..." (Ref. Suet., Caligula, pg. 176, v. 55). If the person who became known to the world as 'Columbus' was familiar with the works of Suetonius, he could have created his alias by using this rather obscure reference by Suetonius.

He tells us of a person called "Areus (Arrius) the Philosopher" (Ref. Suet., Augustus, pg. 98, verse 89). He makes mention of his own grandfather (Arrius) by making mention of his alias identity (Flavius) Josephus. (Ref. Suet., Vespasian, pg. 277, verse 5). His mention of him as "Chrestus" is in the section about Claudius Caesar. (Ref. Suet., Claudius, pg. 197, verse 25).

And he (Suetonius), goes on to joke about "all of the fictional blood that has been shed" (as referred to in the works of Josephus, when Arrius Piso, writing as Josephus, jokes about his fictional character Jesus and the other fictional gang that had died in his stories) and refers [secretly, of course], to the fact that Christians were not 'wasted' by killing them in persecutions. He says; "A good shepherd shears his flock; he does not flay (slay or kill) them." He makes it so that he says that Tiberius had said this. But all professional authors know that authors have always made their characters say what they, themselves, have wanted to say; but could not. Or else put words in the mouths of others to do the very same thing. It may have been an understanding of and between royals that if their descendants want to use them to say things that they cannot say otherwise, that it would be understood among them that they indeed can do so. (Ref. Suet., Tiberius, pg. 126, verse 32)

He jokes about "water being changed to wine" simply by mentioning 'water & wine' together in the same sentence, saying; "...Drinker of wine with water added." (Ref. Suet., Tiberius, pg. 130, verse 42)

Throughout his works, Suetonius jokes about bread dough being mixed with 'unclean' things such as 'mud' and 'blood', and kneaded with (filthy/unclean) 'coin-stained' hands. (Ref. Suetonius, Tiberius, pg. 53, verse 4, and Tiberius, pg. 137, verse 57). Which, is an obvious reference to the Romans making bread with human dung to give to the starving Jews during the time of the war when the Temple was destroyed.

Then, he reveals the true mindset of most royals when he says, "Tiberius did so many other wicked deeds under the pretext (pretense) of reforming public morals – but in reality to gratify his lust for seeing people suffer." And this, is how the majority of royals were. As Arrius Piso, writing as Philo said, there were seen by royals two (main) races of men. And what he meant by that was that there were the royals and the non-royals. And the non-royals were here only to be used by the royals in whatever ways they saw fit. They (the royals) were generally very cruel in their thoughts and deeds. They did not have any reservations about having men die in gladiatorial combat, for instance, merely for their own entertainment. (Ref. Suet., Tiberius, pg. 138, verse 59)

There are many more important statements with hints, clues and evidence for what was really going on. When taken together with all the rest that we know about this, it all not only makes sense, but it shows us much more than we had already known. Anyone who did not know what these Royals were up to would never have known how to interpret what was being written; and therefore, the true meaning remained hidden.

A COMPARISON OF STYLE AND INTENT (Between Flavius Josephus & Suetonius)

Regarding the works of Flavius Josephus and Suetonius, there are things that both of these writers actively do in their writings and that is used to promote various ideas and concepts which are deliberately harmful to human intellect by making these untrue ideas appear to be true and by trying to make them seem valid and real.

(1) Superstition. Both of these authors write throughout their works on subjects that promote superstition and unreasonable beliefs. Josephus is the hands-down champion promoter of superstition, whereas Suetonius makes mention of such things almost in passing. Josephus says things using phrases like "the will of God." And he promotes the idea of 'fate'. Suetonius, on the other hand, talks about what 'sooth-sayers' foretell. Both Josephus and Suetonius promote the idea of 'prophecy'.

(2) Ghosts & 'spirit-beings'. Both promote the idea of ghosts or spirit-beings. These include devil/s and angels.

(3) Heaven/Hell/Afterlife. Both, promote the idea of Heaven and/or Hell, and/or an Afterlife.

(4) Paranormal or Supernatural. Both also promote the idea of the paranormal or a supernatural existence.

All of these things were done in due course to 'deactivate' and slow the thinking processes of the human mind by subverting the mind's base knowledge of the world around it. When there isn't any reliable certitude for the human mind to reference, nothing makes genuine sense anymore. The real or actual thinking process is effectively shut down and a new, different and unrealistic process replaces reality. Which, was the intent of their literary works.

SUETONIUS AS EMPEROR ANTONINUS PIUS

This is an examination of the works of Suetonius' "The Twelve Caesars" so as to find within these texts hints, clues and evidence of Suetonius being aka Emperor Antoninus Pius. This is only a small sampling of material related to this subject and should not be taken as the total amount of evidence for this deduction.

What we will be examining is only some evidence from the works of Suetonius himself. There is other evidence elsewhere that also will be examined later and perhaps in conjunction with this evidence. It was Abelard Reuchlin who had first written about Suetonius and the Emperor Antoninus Pius actually being one and the same person. We will also eventually examine what he had to say about this.

As Suetonius, the author, his name was Gaius Suetonius Tranquillus. His father's name was supposed to have been Suetonius Laetus, a tribune of the people, who served with the Thirteenth Legion in a military campaign under Otho. [Ref. Suetonius, pg. 260, Otho, verses 9 & 10] However, upon further examination, we discover the other names used by this person and we find out who he (Antoninus) and his father (Rufus Corelius) really were, as well as his mother (Claudia Phoebe aka Pompeia Plotina) and her second husband (Emperor Trajan aka Pudens), and Suetonius' half-brother Arrian, who wrote histories as Arrian and Appian as well as other works.

Here are some items in the works of Suetonius that point to him as Emperor Antoninus Pius:

(1) He was very close to the Emperor Hadrian. A fact that is expressed in Suetonius' work, and when taken with the historical account of how the Emperor Antoninus Pius was chosen to succeed Hadrian, as well as the time when Suetonius had written his works and when Antoninus Pius became Emperor, the correlation can be seen. It becomes much clearer when the total weight of evidence is introduced. See an example of Suetonius' talking about his closeness and fondness for Hadrian below. In places, it appears that he, Suetonius is very nearly bragging if not actually doing so. Throughout his work "The Twelve Caesars," he makes certain to make the Caesars appear to be larger than life and so greatly superior to the average man.

He is the person, in fact, that makes the diametrical distinction between the common man and Caesar by giving us the phrase; "Hail Caesar! We (common men) who are about to die (in gladiatorial combat), salute you!" As if it were an honor to have the total of one's life come to an end simply to entertain the Emperor! (Ref. Suet., pg. 195, Claudius, verse 21) This is something that he would want for himself, if he, were an Emperor. To be honored in such a way that common men would gladly lay down their lives for him!

(2) When referring to the 'Julian' Caesars, he very cleverly phrases the statement so as to be inclusive. Meaning it could be taken two ways. One way is that he could be talking of the Julian Caesars, or the other way is that he could be speaking of both himself and the Julians as being Caesars! He says; "... of which we Caesars are a branch (of the Marcii)." (Ref. Suet., pg. 11, Julius Caesar, verse 6)

(3) Suetonius states that he once owned a statuette of Augustus (presumably, for those who know who he really is, he is saying that this was passed down to him from within his own family), and he says that he had then presented it to Hadrian. So, here we have Suetonius, presenting Hadrian with a statuette of Augustus. He either genuinely admires and respects Hadrian or he was trying to get on his good side; possibly in order to be considered by him as his successor. (Ref. Suet., pg. 53, Augustus, verse 7)

(4) Suetonius talks about Cleopatra as "the most famous" of Julius Caesar's mistresses, and as being so wonderful as the Queen of Egypt. (Ref. Suet., pg. 32, Julius Caesar, verse 52) When we trace his ancestry back via his mother, we find that Cleopatra was his ancestor! And this is what we find in ancient history as a rule. These authors were building up the glory of their own ancestors, as this also made them appear to be

great and glorious as well (especially either in their other personifications, and/or when you realize just who they, the authors really were!).

(5) His (Suetonius' aka Antoninus Pius), half-brother was the son of the Emperor Trajan (via a wife prior to his marriage to Claudia Phoebe, according to research notes), and Trajan's ancestry can be traced back to Augustus. And when we view the true relationship between the various Emperors, we can see just how tightly the reigns of power over Rome were kept within the family. Which, means that the possibility was nil that anyone other than a close family member would ever be chosen as Emperor. No way at all. Only one of those who were of a close branch to previous Emperors could ever be chosen as Emperor. And Suetonius, aka Antoninus Pius was of that family. By the way, he, Suetonius/Antoninus Pius had many alias names. And that is another aspect of this that we will have to examine to give the full weight to all of this evidence.

(6) Knowing what we already do about the fact that the ancient royals had tight control over all that was written for public consumption and, again, how tightly they held the reigns of power – how is it that Suetonius could not only have access to the royal archives, but also get his works published unless he was one of them? The answer, of course, is that he was one of them.

(7) He makes a rather strange statement about the name "Caesar," saying that the 'Aesar' portion in Etruscan means "God," and that the 'C' was the Roman 100. (Ref., Augustus, pg. 104, verse 97) And he says other things that only one of the Caesars would have known! He knows the family tree intimately, for instance. That is something, to which the family would never allow access to any outsider.

Again, for those readers who may not yet understand why it is that it was important for these people to write using alias name – the reason is again explained. It was in order to create the illusion that (a) anyone could write a book and have it become famous or well-known, when the truth of the matter is that no one could do this except for the royals, and (b) because another part of this illusion includes making it appear that many different people were writing.

(8) He speaks of Aeneas the Trojan hero, who was an ancestor of the Julians (in a verse about Nero). But Aeneas and the other ancient Trojan kings were also Suetonius' ancestors in several ways! Also, by making mention of 'Aeneas' he both alludes to and honors Seneca and those of that branch of his family. (Ref. Suet., pg. 232, verse 39)

(9) Suetonius had Nero's notebooks and loose pages as he states in an almost bragging way – as if he is just bursting to say that he is really Emperor and that is why he enjoyed all of the very special reserved privileges! How did Suetonius get these? They were passed down to him by those in Suetonius' own family who had taken them when Nero had been killed.! (Ref. Suet., 239, verse 52)

FLAVIUS JOSEPHUS WAS REALLY ARRIUS PISO (Following the Trail)

From the family of Vespasian to the Pisos: The tie-in is that Arria the Elder was married to the emperor Vespasian's brother (before Vespasian became emperor). He was T. Flavius Sabinus.

From this relationship we find the connection to the alias names of the Pisos as "Paetus". Quoting from "The True Authorship of the New Testament," by Abelard Reuchlin; "Vespasian relied upon Piso because he was grandson of his own brother - Vespasian's brother, T. Flavius Sabinus, had married Arria Sr. (i.e., Arria the Elder), who was Piso's maternal grandmother. Piso's identity as thus also a Flavian is decipherable from the appearance in the Flavian family line of L. Caesennius Paetus (Townsend, Gavin, 'Some Flavian Connections', Journal of Roman Studies, LI. 54, 62, 1961). That was an alias (like Thrasea Paetus) of Piso's father, L. Calpurnius Piso [Note: we now know Arrius Piso's father to have been Gaius Calpurnius Piso who was executed by Nero]. See page 20 supra, wherein Piso himself also is mentioned as a Caesennius Paetus. That is the true reason Piso used the literary pseudonym of Flavius; it was not because of his alleged - but untrue and hardly necessary - adoption by Emperor Flavius Vespasian. He was in fact (already, technically) a Flavian (via inherited name usage)."

This information leads us to:

(1) The son of Thrasea Paetus/Gaius Calpurnius Piso (who is unnamed in history). And then to…

(2) Flavius Josephus, and to…

(3) Montanus, as another alias name of Arrius Piso.

There are elements of this that are given in "The True Authorship of the New Testament" that may not be necessary to repeat here in detail such as how it is that Thrasea Paetus and Arria are seen as really being

Gaius Piso and his wife. You can find that with the use of that booklet and your own research.

Instead, we will try to stick to the main issue here rather than side-track or let this get too confusing for you the reader/researcher. Let's concentrate upon what you need to know in order to 'follow the trail' from one alias name to the next. To fill in the gaps and further deduce from this information, we examine more closely the family of Thrasea Paetus and both of the Arrias (Arria the Elder and Arria the Younger). From this, we find the daughter of Arria the Younger as one "Fannia". "Fannia" too, is an alias name. Her real name was used to make her alias name. She was Flavia Arria. The feminine form of "Flavius", and the name of her mother and grandmother -Arria. They used the "F" in "Flavia" as an initial and left it in front of her Arria name and changed the 'r's in her name to 'n's (which is explained by the use of Royal Language). This rendered the alias name of "Fannia" (F. Annia).

Her brother, likewise also already carried/used the Flavius name and he would have the masculine form of his mother's name and therefore would be "Arrius." And now we have the "Arrius" portion of his name. But we will also find much more confirmation of this as we research and deduce further. Quoting from "The True Authorship of the New Testament,"; "Likewise "Montanus" (the mountain?) "is spared out of consideration for his father [having died on order of Nero]" when Thrasea Paetus is killed." (pg. 20). Ref. Tacitus, Annals, XVI. 33., Loeb Classical Library edition. See the Bibliographical Index in the Letters of Pliny the Younger (Letters and Panegyricus), Loeb Classical Library edition, for data on; Thrasea Paetus, Arria the Elder, Arria the Younger, Fannia, Montanus and Arrius Antoninus. Note that Arria the Younger is called "Caecina ANNIA" also in history. Ref. Tacitus, The Annals, Book XVI, XXXIV, pg. 387, Loeb edition.

This next section is about "Evidence". Some of the items from above may be repeated here for various reasons; emphasis, clarification or because it also relates to other items that we are examining here. First of all, this particular subject really requires a full book length treatise to illustrate it fully - or ideally, several books which explore the whole thing in detail. So we will do the best that we can here.

One of the first things that come to mind in trying to explain this is just "where to start?" And next is the reality of the fact that the average reader is unprepared and not fully familiar with primary information that they would need in order to fully comprehend what would be stated regarding this. So, there is an extreme disadvantage here right from the start. Because of this, it would probably be best to just give a "list" of the various proofs that (1) Flavius Josephus was really Arrius Piso, and (2) Arrius Piso was/played "Jesus" in the New Testament. In terms of Arrius Calpurnius Piso himself, he indeed made certain that his full and real name was never to be found anywhere that was obvious in history - therefore hiding his true identity from everyone but a limited few.

To restate this, the name "Arrius Calpurnius Piso" is not found in any outright fashion in ancient Roman history. But, it can be deduced and therefore reconstructed, because it is found in parts or 'chopped up' here and there. It is a matter of putting all of the 'parts' together to get his true full name. Remember, this name was deliberately hidden and for an express purpose. Abelard Reuchlin puts it this way; "He does not appear (in history) as Arius Calpurnius Piso. His true identity is decipherable only by reconstruction." When his true name and identity are discovered and known the rest starts to fall into place and the truth unravels. The easiest way to find that "Arrius Calpurnius Piso" is his real name, is to find him as (C.) Caesennius Paetus when his father as Thrasea Paetus is found out to really be Gaius Calpurnius Piso, who was put to death (by order of suicide) by Nero in 65 CE.

At that point, you know that he is the son of Gaius Calpurnius Piso, and that therefore the "Calpurnius Piso" part of his real/true name becomes known. From there one may deduce from information available in ancient history and in articles dealing with specifics of it that his first name was "Arrius" as the masculine form of his mother's name (Arria). You may well wish to note that the Jewish historic commentary tries to point this out with the "Pantera" riddle. This will be explained in more detail later on. And one may also wish to note that Arrius Calpurnius Piso's real name was not "Gaius Calpurnius Piso, Jr.", as he just assumes that as an alter or alias name for the specific purpose of indicating that he was the son of Gaius Calpurnius Piso. His true name is the one that people in his family knew him as and referred to him - and as we go forward here, it will become more and more apparent that his name was indeed "Arrius".

One of the best proofs for Flavius Josephus being the primary author of the Gospels and the inventor of "Jesus" is simply the correlations that are found between the works of Flavius Josephus and the New Testament itself. Those correlations will be made available to the public in the upcoming years. It is quite fortunate for us that the Romans were not the only ones who were leaving records and information of the people and history in those times.

The Jews (Pharisees), whom Rome was at war with over this very issue likewise left us what information that they could within their particular circumstance. Like the Romans, they too used what we refer to as 'royal language' as they could not write about this openly either and had to resort to hints, riddles and clues as well. But now that we know just how to read that 'royal language', we can also read what they had written - just as they wrote it and intended it to be read by those whom could do so.

Because of what this reveals, it demonstrates to us that history (especially ancient history) as we think we know it, did not happen in the way in which we had previously thought that it had and we must now expect that more and more evidence likewise will be found that is consistent with the way in which it did happen.

What this also means is that because the ancient authors were in complete control of what kind of evidence (in terms of their literary creations) and how much of various facts and information that they would give to us, we more or less find ourselves at their virtual 'mercy' as far as just what evidence they chose to leave to us for the purpose of finding out the real truth of matters in ancient history. And this should be considered when one is expecting to find one type of evidence or another. But this also means that what was left, was left to us in what may be called 'near pristine' condition as far as what we find in the original texts - and that is much better than what we had previously thought we had in terms of what texts and info we had from those times. What is meant by this is that they did not write about just anyone, all of the people who were mentioned in history were relatives of theirs' whether this was disguised by the use of an alias name or not. There were not a lot of different (common) people writing, these were royals. Which, makes identifying just who wrote what, that much more easier for us.

Now, a bit about Josephus and Joseph the father of Jesus. Jesus' father is Joseph (Josephus), his mother is not impregnated by a mere mortal man, but rather by "God." "God" came to mean something different to us in this time than it did to those authors living in those times. "God" had previously been a generic title inherited and used by Kings and other rulers. But because we (as a society) do not know this today, in our own time, we tend to think that Jesus' mother had to be impregnated by "God" and that "God" could not also be her husband (figuratively speaking... remember, we are talking about a fictional story). Josephus, as "Joseph", the father of Jesus was actually a High Priest, but he was also a ruler/king (kings were sometimes called 'governors' in ancient history - which is something recently revealed by our research).

However, as just stated, he (Josephus/Arrius Piso) would theoretically not actually have to be a king or ruler to use the inherited name/title "God", if he was of the/a royal lineage. He would just have it as a "birthright" to use when and how he pleased - which, is precisely what he did. Another thing that is quite telling about the Piso family and their close relatives is that the Piso family had a history of being 'governors' of Syria. That is to say in actuality, kings installed there by Rome. Syria was generally a region that was ruled over by the Pisos for many generations consecutively, with perhaps a close relative of theirs stepping in as a figurehead occasionally. But primarily, Syria was the territory of the Pisos for a very long expanse of time. The Pisos and Syria in ancient history had very nearly become synonymous with each other - and so, this is another way of knowing what is being said regarding the Pisos in a secretive way.

There is a place where "Jesus" is said to have been "famous" in Syria, for instance. It wasn't "Jesus", most certainly not, who was "famous" in Syria, but rather the person who was playing Jesus in the New Testament (Ref. Matt. 4:24, "Jesus" famous or well-known in Syria). As Caesennius Paetus, Arrius Piso was the governor of Syria (Ref. Flavius Josephus, Jewish War II, VII, 59, Whiston translation; and also "The True Authorship of the New Testament", by Abelard Reuchlin, pg. 20). Reuchlin says; Then Caesennius Paetus appears as governor of Syria, but because he is still Caesennius, he is still Josephus." As Claudius Aristion "he was called the "leading citizen" of Ephesus (Ref. Pliny,VI.31.3.). Ephesus, was the Chief City of the Roman province of Asia which was to the South West of Bithynia. We also find him as Flavius Archippus who was supposedly a philosopher whom emperor Domitian commended to Pliny the Younger (under Pliny's alter name/identity of Lappius Maximus. The emperor ordered Pliny to "buy" Flavius Archippus/Arrius Piso a farm near Prusa (in Bithynia) and out of public funds it would appear, or else by ruthless means to obtain this farm property. The people of Prusa (supposedly) voted to put up a statue as tribute to him (Flavius Archippus aka Josephus/Arrius Piso).

Now, if we could just find one of these statues or other likeness of Piso from his time we would really have something to show what he looked like. But for now, let's follow Arrius Piso through his alias names. Here is the order in which we will use so as to keep this organized in a way that will be easier for the reader to understand and to follow:

1. (C.) CAESENNIUS PAETUS leads us to Arrius Calpurnius Piso.

2. ARRIUS CALPURNIUS PISO (his real name) leads us to Montanus.

3. MONTANUS leads us to Arrius Antoninus.

4. ARRIUS ANTONINUS leads us to Arrius Verus.

5. ARRIUS VERUS leads us to Annius Gallus.

6. ANNIUS GALLUS leads us to Cestius Gallus.

7. CESTIUS GALLUS leads us to Gessius Florus.

8. GESSIUS FLORUS leads us to Antoninus Primus.

9. ANTONIUS PRIMUS.

1. (C.) CAESENNIUS PAETUS

We have already examined (C.) Caesennius Paetus and will have references for that and other items here at the end of this article. So, we can go on to examine Arrius Calpurnius Piso.

2. ARRIUS CALPURNIUS PISO

Arrius Calpurnius Piso definitely had many, many more alias names. But for now it is important to know these names before going on to the rest. Below you will find examples of his "Arrius" name used both in the history of his time and in the New Testament as well:

(a) He is "Arrius" as Arrius Antoninus, in the history of his time.

(b) He is Areios/Arrius as the god Mars incarnate and is mentioned as the god Mars throughout the works of Juvenal (Loeb edition).

(c) He is "Arrius" (Annius) as the brother of Flavia Arria (i.e. Fannia).

(d) He is "Arrius", because as Jesus he is called by the Jews "ben Pantera", meaning that he is "son of his mother" (Arria). The Jews were pointing out that his name was "Arrius" as the masculine form of his mother's name (Arria). One of the other things that we found in our research of royal language is that "T" and "TH" were often switched or used interchangeably. So, "Pantera" (or "Pentera") could also be "PenTHera", which is "mother" (i.e., his mother, "Arria"). Knowing this shows us that "ben PenTHera", means "son of mother" (Arria). The Jews say that he is "son of mother", so that when one finds out that "Jesus" was really being played by the person who invented him, and we know that person to be Josephus and/or even (C.) Caesennius Paetus, that we would be pointed to his mother so that we could find his name as being "Arrius" as the masculine form of his mother's name.

Other things that the Jews knew and used were the hints and clues given by the authors of the New Testament themselves! The Greek word "PenTHera" for "mother" is in Mark 1:30, Matt. 8.14, Luke 4:38. In Matthew 12:48, Jesus (the person who was playing him rather) says; "Who is my mother?" He is asking a question, a question that of course to which the average person thinks that they know the answer - "Mary" ("Mary" is another form/spelling of "Arria"), but it is a deceptive one. The question is asked by him, Arrius Piso, to point towards his own mother as the source of his real name of Arrius... and so more is said in the form of questions. Matt. 13:55; "Is not his (Jesus/Arrius Piso) mother called "Mary?" If his name is "Arrius" as the masculine form of "Arria" (his mother), then his sister would also have the same name as his mother, i.e. "Arria". Her name was hidden in history by simply changing the r's to n's, and by putting the initial of her first name ("F") in front of her name instead of spelling it out ("Flavia").

(e) As Jesus, he is the "Lamb", and the word for lamb is "Arnius" in Greek and in the royal language it is seen as "Arrius" because r's and n's are interchangeable (Ref. John 1:29, Greek/English Interlinear New Testament).

(f) His name is inserted into the New Testament by several means. One of which is by the mention of the marketplace of "Appius", as in the royal language r's and p's are interchangeable to render the name "Arrius" (Acts 28:15, Greek/English Interlinear New Testament).

(g) In the Revelations, 6:6, "Arrius" is inserted by mentioning the word "denARIUS." And in his true ingenious style the author of the Revelations (Julius Calpurnius Piso) also makes this secretly as a question. And the reason we know this is that, "den" means "did not", and so it actually reads; "did not Arrius?" And when one knows this, we also get to read the question with the inferred words to give the full question of; "Did not Arrius (Piso) do/create it?" This is sheer genius. Now, with the combined knowledge that (C.) Caesennius Paetus was an alias name of Arrius Calpurnius Piso, we now go on to examine the name Montanus in comparison with what we already know.

3. MONTANUS

Well, we have already found that Thrasea Paetus and Caesennius Paetus were alias names of Gaius Calpurnius Piso and his son Arrius Calpurnius Piso because of the many factors involved with each and their other family members. Thrasea Paetus and Caesennius Paetus were not just alias names, but were also "composites" for the real persons behind the names. And so, we look to find other similar composites that may be telling and we find the same similarity in the name and figure of "Montanus". So, we examine this critically.

Why "Montanus" for an alias name of Arrius Piso? One of the reasons could be because he saw himself as a large immovable object such as a large hill or mountain. And he saw himself as the god Mars, who was the God of War, incarnate. And then he could also joke about this in the New Testament where "Mar's Hill" is mentioned - because "Mar's Hill" in Greek is "Areios Pagos" And a "mount" (like Mount Olympus), a large hill or mountain in Greek is "Pagos", so here we have "Areios (Arrius) Mountain/Montanus". But "pagos" can also be "opos" ("ippos" phonetically in Greek) when viewing it in royal language and "ip(p)os" is "horse" or "beast" which is also what Arrius Piso was referred to. "Ippos" is the name "Piso" rearranged, and in the Revelations, Julius Calpurnius Piso refers to his father (Arrius) as "the Beast". So, to say "Mar's Hill" we could say in our meaning in Greek "Arrius Ippos/Piso" (Ref. Acts 17:19 and 17:22).

A more detailed explanation of things not explained more fully here will be found in other works on this subject. There is also another joke in the New Testament where as Jesus, he (Arrius Piso) is slyly referred to as a "Mountain" (John 4:21). But bear in mind that many of these jokes and names cannot be seen in translated or interpreted versions of the New Testament. For the average person to 'see' these, they would have to use a good Greek/English Interlinear New Testament. Or, they would have to be able to read the Greek language of that time and they would have to go to the earliest known Greek New Testament texts and translate the words in order to see/read this. In any case, this particular joke is rather interesting as it shows the author clearly "talking out of the side of his mouth."

In John 4:21, Jesus (Arrius Piso) says; "Woman, believe me, the hour is coming when you shall worship the (ancestral) Father neither in (the form of) this mountain ("Montanus", i.e. Arrius Piso), nor in Jerusalem." He is saying more than one thing here. He is referring to himself as "this mountain", that is himself as "the mountain" because he is "Montanus." The reason he says that she will not worship the (ancestral) Father (i.e. "god", whom was the original "god", that being Pharaoh Adamenhept I from whom Arrius Piso derives his 'power' and inherited name/title of "god") in Jerusalem is because he was pointing to the fact that Jerusalem by that time had been destroyed. It was later than 70 CE when this was being written.

And he is also saying that the day will eventually come, when Christianity will end. There is more and more evidence pointing towards Arrius Piso's son Julius Piso having a great concern about Christianity, and that they, as the authors should make statements in the New Testament that will allow humanity to one day find out the truth about all of this. And so, it appears that statements referring to the end of Christianity that were inserted into the New Testament were done to appease this son (Julius) of Arrius Piso.

In Pliny (the works of Pliny the Younger), we find "Montanus" as a senator. From the Bibliographical Index in the works of Pliny the Younger (Loeb Classical Library edition): "Montanus, unknown senator; letters on monument to freedman Pallas and honors voted him" (VII. 29; VIII. 6).

We also see as we follow the trail, all of these who were involved in this fraud as well (such as Pliny the Younger). And we find, eventually, that this involved all of the Roman authors and we also find them to be closely related to each other - the Roman emperors and those who were writing their histories. This should make some people sit up and take notice.

"Montanus" was spared (by Nero) out of consideration for his father (Gaius Piso, who was forced to commit suicide by Nero), with the proviso (provision) that his official career should not be continued" (Ref. Tacitus, Annals, Book XVI, XXXIII, pg. 387, Loeb). "Montanus" is also mentioned in many other places. Now knowing that "Montanus" is Arrius Piso, we continue looking for "Arrius" and we now find "Arrius Antoninus."

4. ARRIUS ANTONINUS

Why the alias name of Arrius Antoninus? We have already found his name as "Arrius". So, we wonder why "Antoninus"? We have found examples of other alias names that were used which incorporated the use of component parts of other names and/or initials or abbreviations in some instances to create alias names/identities. And it may well be further found that there were indeed various purposes involved for the use of alias names and their component parts as yet not fully recognized, such as the use of these as "indicators" of ancestry. We are finding out more and more about these things all of the time.

Now we look at "Antoninus" and find an obvious indication of descent from the Antonii line - and as we will find as we go along, this was intentional. It was given as an indication that Arrius Piso was indeed descended from Marc Antony himself. And that explains the "Antoni" portion of the invented name. When one stops to think of all of this it is truly amazing that all of this was done and remained hidden from the public for so long - but there were a variety of methods and means used by them specifically for that purpose. Even fooling the brightest of scholars up to this time. But now this information is known to many and is even more available to everyone via the Internet. And so, it is our hope that the "Dark Age" which has resulted from the work of those ancient royals will now soon end.

Remembering that the purpose of these alias names and also realizing that great pains were taken specifically to hide these things, and not to make them appear obvious (except in small bits and pieces), while likewise bearing in mind that they... the authors were most ingenious, used the royal language, etc., we can easily envision them making "double use" of letters already used in these names as just another way of further hiding hints, clues and other info.

In the alias name "Antoninus" we find the use of "ninus". What is "ninus"? "Ninus" is a secret title or nickname. It is really the Greek "nini", which is "baby" or infant - which, in reality refers to, indicates and confirms that this person was "a baby" - the baby JESUS! Julius Piso called his father a "dragon" in the Revelations. That was because by doing so he was also pointing out that his father was "a baby boy" as that is what the word used for dragon refers to - he too was saying that his father, Arrius Piso, was JESUS!

Let's take a moment to review what we have found so far. We found that Flavius Josephus was really just a penname of Arrius Calpurnius Piso, and that Arrius Piso had played the fictional character "Jesus" in the New Testament story. We also found that Tacitus, the historian, was involved in this fraud as well as Pliny the Younger. It is sincerely hoped that now as all of this is known that ancient history will NEVER be viewed again in the same way as it has for nearly 2000 years up to now.

How deluded must a person be to not recognize that this is the true way in which all of this had happened? Who could read and investigate all of this and say that it is merely a coincidence? No one at all we should think, as long as they have a working brain, basic information - and are honest with themselves. They should realize that emotionalism does not enter into serious objective study of this subject.

And as far as the premise of "Jesus" being good, etc., because all of that is dependent upon the information about "Jesus" being a real person and not an invented composite character - we also realize that this is not true either. That idea or concept of Jesus as being real was only a part of the fraud itself.

5. ARRIUS VARUS

Now why "Arrius Varus" as an alias? Well, it gives Arrius a chance to use his real name of "Arrius", and that is one reason. But another is because he can really play with and use this alias while honoring himself and his descendants.

The name "Varus" is the Roman form of the Egyptian "Veru," meaning "great men", but when used as a 'name' of an individual it means that the man who has and uses the name is a "great man". As Arrius Verus, he is found as the founding ancestor of the later great Roman family - the "Annii Anicii." "Annius" and "Arrius" are the same as explained previously. And he (Arrius Piso) is also the founder of the "Annii Verii." Using the royal language one sees in this alias name another name that was used - "Severus." Let's look at this.

"Arrius Verus" (vowels were interchangeable always because they are seen as not actually being there, i.e., 'invisible' or tentative, excepting as to be used to make names appear to readers to be different), the 's' from Arrius is given a vowel ("e") to bind it to "Verus", thus rendering

"Severus". This is a name used by Arrius Piso's son Julius Piso as a commander of the Roman forces against the Jews in the Bar Cochba revolt.

Tacitus says; "As Antonius (that is, "Antonius Primus") hurried forward some dispatchments from the cohorts and part of the cavalry to invade Italy, he was accompanied by Arrius Varus…"He was "accompanied" by Arrius Varus, in this instance, because he was one and the same person. Naturally, wherever Antonius Primus went, Arrius Varus was sure to go… as they are the same person! Are you starting to understand just how ancient history was REALLY written? We hope so.

In the same passage, Tacitus says; "However, Antonius (Primus) and Varus (of course!) occupied Aquileia…" Yes, they were BOTH there, in one place, and in one body! Another interesting thing that Tacitus does is to call "Antonius Primus" - "Primus Antonius". One would think the purpose that Tacitus had in mind was to further confuse/confound the reader into thinking that he is speaking of two different persons, just as he does in calling Arrius Piso several different (alias) names. He is very actively participating in this fraud (Ref. Tacitus, II, Histories, Book III, VI, pg. 337, Loeb Classical Library edition).

6. ANNIUS GALLUS

We will start to see proof that the other historians of the time were also very actively involved in this fraud as well. This name is particularly telling when we find just which authors of the day had used this alias name to refer to Arrius Piso.

As if the circle has not been completed by this point, still there is more to bring this all around "full circle" again. We know by now that "Annius" is just another spelling of "Arrius", so we look for "Gallus." Turning now to Suetonius we find that the person who killed the emperor Vitellius was none other than our "friend" Antonius Primus, and he is called "Gallus" thereby saying that he is a ("c" word for male chicken) "rooster" and a person from Gaul. By the way, "Gallus" is also another way of using the "Pollio" name that Arrius Piso had also inherited, as they are the same in meaning. They both refer to the "rooster" and in turn, the "rooster" is also a secret way of alluding to the Phoenix, which one finds to be synonymous with the phallic symbol and in meaning, "god." So, in a very hidden way, calling Arrius "Gallus" is in fact saying or acknowledging him to be "god."

As we have already noted that Suetonius is among the list of authors who were contributing to this fraud, we also find "Annius Gallus" in Plutarch's "Lives" under "Otho." And Juvenal also makes mention of a "Gallus" in his works (Juvenal, VII. 144, Loeb). Tacitus did not miss the chance to use this alias name of Arrius Piso either. See: Tacitus, II, Histories, Book II, XLIV, pg. 233; and Tacitus, II, Histories, Book II, XXXIII, pg. 215; as well as Tacitus, II, Histories, Book II, XI; and Tacitus, II, Histories, Book I, LXXXVII, pg.151. "Annius Gallus" by now should be easy to see as an alias name of Arrius Piso and should be seen as "Arrius Gallus". This is a connecting/affirming alias name that allows the reader who is able to deduce things such as this and who has the ability to make use of their knowledge of the 'royal language' to make the affirmation and connection to the fact that "Cestius Gallus" also was an alias name of Arrius Piso. This is, after all, a "trail" that was left to follow... and so, we have added Plutarch, Juvenal and Suetonius to our list of participants in the fraud.

7. & 8. CESTIUS GALLUS & GESSIUS FLORUS

We will look at both of these in comparison to each other to help bring forth a better understanding of the other alias names that have been listed and those that we are yet to find out about. Why Gessius Florus? He disguises an ancestral name which is "Cassius," as "Gessius" and attaches "FL" from "Flavius," while enjoying the name/title of (H) orus - as the Egyptian god which is reborn/incarnate now in the form of Arrius Piso. As Gessius Florus, he is a Roman procurator in Judea and is the cause of the Jewish revolt at that time. Writing as Josephus, Arrius Piso tries to make it appear that Gessius Florus is a different person from Cestius Gallus, but the name Cestius Gallus is telling us differently. The name "Cestius" is the same as "Gessius" as seen in royal language because "C" and "G" are interchangeable to the point of being exactly the same anyway. And "S" and "T" are used in the same manner.

While we are on the subject of Arrius Piso and his use of the name "Gallus" and that being another way of saying/using his inherited name of "Pollio," we should not forget another name by which he was known; that of "Annius Pollio." Again, the reader by this time should be used to 'seeing' the "Annius" name as "Arrius" and now we see the use of the name that came down to him from many of his ancestors and relatives - "Pollio." Arrius Piso as "Annius Pollio" is incriminated in the Pisonian Conspiracy (plot) against Nero and was sent into exile. Which is exactly what happened to him under other alias names! Refer to the article "Domitius Corbulo" by Sir Ronald Syme in the JRS (Journal of Roman Studies), post 1969; and also Tacitus, Annals, XVI, 30, 3.; and Tacitus, Annals, XVI, 21, I. Arrius Piso as "Annius Pollio" was sentenced to exile (in Tacitus, Annals, Book XV, LXXI, pg. 329, Loeb).

And by the way, the Roman writer Martial mentions Cestius Gallus in his works (Ref. Martial, XLII, 2., Loeb). Add Martial to our list of participants in the fraud (actually, as has already been mentioned, all that was written at that time for public consumption was controlled by the Roman royal authorities. All of those authors were a part of that oligarchy in one way or another. And the name "Gallus" is very telling because a) it is another way of saying "Poll(I)o", which is an ancestral name of the Flavians, and b) because they both mean chicken or "fowl" in general, as previously stated. Moreover, c) chicken or fowl refers to the winged phallus that Jesus also was synonymous with, and d) Arrius Piso as Antonius Primus is supposed to have been born in Gaul (and so can be referred to as "Gallus") according to Suetonius, and e) Suetonius adds that as a boy, Antonius Primus had the "nickname" (alias name) of "becko"(rooster's beak). And further, f) as you can see, this and other alias names of Arrius Piso lead us to yet another alias - that of "Antonius Primus."

9. ANTONIUS PRIMUS

Why "Antonius Primus" as an alias name for Arrius Piso? Well, for one thing we were led to this name by the process of logical deduction. And here, we find the use and emphasis of the "Antonius" name again. And "Primus" is used because he considered himself the "prime" one or prime source (which he was, because he made himself so), and numero uno - number "1", the big shot.

He was/is the "key" to finding out about all of the rest of this. No one gets to anything of any real consequence regarding this unless they first "go through Arrius Calpurnius Piso." One needs to know that Arrius Piso used many other alias names (more than anyone else that could be found!), and as a result that, the rest of this begins to comes out. The name "Antonius Primus" was used by Arrius Piso himself in the works that he wrote as Flavius Josephus, and that name is also found used in reference to him (Arrius Piso) in the works of Suetonius, and in Tacitus (Ref. Tacitus, II, Histories, Book II, LXXXVI, pg. 131, Loeb).

It seems that one way that they reconciled to themselves the use of alias for the purpose of deception was to think of them as "nicknames" - nicknames for which only they were fully aware of the full and true meanings. Arrius Piso was rather proud of his ancestry and particularly that of his descent from Marc Antony. His ancestry from Marc Antony has been reconstructed by us researchers of the New Classical Scholarship and we were able to do this because he made certain that it was given out in bits and pieces for those who were able to connect the dots that had been left, and then to figure it out by deduction.

NOTES & REFERENCES

A short stemma for Caesennius Paetus and family:
C. Caecina Paetus
M. Arria the Elder
|
Caecina Arria the Younger
M. Thrasea Paetus
|
Fannia
M. Helvidius Priscus

Ref. "Domitius Corbulo", Ronald Syme, JRS. Pliny the Younger, Epp. III, 16, 7ff. Tacitus, Annals, Book XVI, XXXIV, pg. 387, Loeb. Thrasea Paetus' wife Arria the Younger was a relative of Persius the Poet. Ref. Suetonius, "Lives of Illustrious Men", "On Poets - Persius", pg. 497, 499.

Tacitus is careful not to mention that Thrasea Paetus and Arria also had a son (Arrius Piso). He says; "To touch Nero with shame for his infamies was an idle dream, and it was much more to be feared that he (Nero) would exercise his cruelty on Thrasea's wife, his daughter, and other objects of his affection." He does not mention son directly, but leaves open the possibility that one (or more) might exist.

Then, to further hide the existence of this son (Arrius) Tacitus says; "Arria, who aspired to follow her husband's ending and the precedent set by her mother and namesake, he (Thrasea Paetus) advised (her) to keep her life and not to deprive the child of their union of HER one support." He could say this because Arrius was in exile! And that meant that he was not there to support his sister - as it also implies that Fannia did not or would not have a husband at that time (Ref. Tacitus, Annals, Book XVI, XXVI).

There is quite a bit of information about this family in an article titled "People in Pliny", by Ronald Syme, JRS (Journal of Roman Studies), 1968-69, pg. 144, 146, 148. Such as;

(1) A. Caecina Paetus, suff. 37 CE, of Patavium.

(2) P. Clodius Thrasea Paetus (also of Patavium), who married the daughter of the above A. Caecina Paetus. (3) Arria the Younger as wife of Thrasea Paetus.

(4) C. Fannius (Arrius Piso) as barrister who wrote the biographies of Nero's victims. To quote: "Supposed relative of Fannia, the daughter of Patavine (P. Clodius) Thrasea Paetus by marriage with Arria, the daughter of A. Caecina Paetus (suff. 37), cf. Groag in PIR-2, F 116." Syme here says; "Why she should be called "Fannia", no clue." He is right, one would think a daughter of an "Arria" would carry the name of her own mother - somewhere. It is there. She is "F." Arria/Annia w/ r's as n's.

Ref. for Thrasea Paetus and C. Caecina Paetus; "Domitius Corbulo," by Ronald Syme, JRS, (post 1969). His source was Pliny the Younger, Epp. III, 16. 7 ff.

As Caesennius Paetus, Arrius Piso married Vespasian's niece, who was probably his first wife (Ref. "Some Flavian Connections", Gavin Townend, JRS (Journal of Roman Studies), 1961. Also see Syme, "Tacitus", 595, n5). Ref. for Caecina Paetus and Arria the Elder; Dio Cassius, 7. 407f.

Polla, the wife of Lucan the Poet is referred to as "Queen" by Martial. Note that "Polla" is the feminine form of "Pollo/Pollio" (Martial, Book X, LXIV, Loeb).

Arria mentioned by Martial (I. XIII). Pliny the Younger mentions Arria in Epist. III, 16.3. Tacitus speaks of Arria (Tacitus, Annals, XVI). "Thrasea" is mentioned in Juvenal (Juvenal, V.36, Loeb). Thrasea Paetus, Arria the Elder, Arria the Younger, and Fannia are all mentioned in the Annals of Tacitus; Book XVI, XXIV, pg. 373; Book XVI, XXV, pg. 375-377; Book XVI, XXVIII, pg. 379-381; Book XVI, XXXIV, pg. 387. Read through books: XVI,XXIV, XXV, XXVI, XXVII, XXIX, XXXIII, XXXIV, XXXV (Loeb).

In Appian's Roman History, there is C. Philo Caesennius (Paetus). "Paetus" is inferred the same way that "Piso" would be when the name "Frugi" is used (Appian, Roman History, IV. 27, Loeb). Note that it has been discovered that Arrius Piso wrote as Philo of Alexandria, and so it is natural to find "Philo" as another alias of his or used to produce one. Arrius Piso wrote as Philo for several reasons, not the least of which to historicize characters and make mention of those which he wished to emphasize. Case in point, (Pontius) Pilate (Ref. Philo, Vol. X, "The Embassy to Gaius (Caligula)," pg. 151,153, Loeb). History records that both Arria the Younger and Fannia were alive when Nerva became emperor in 96 CE. They had been in exile under Emperor Domitian. Arrius Piso as "Caesennius Paetus" was the governor (president/king) of Syria, as several of the Piso ancestry were noted for being "governors of Syria" (Ref. Flavius Josephus, Jewish Wars, II, VII. 59; or Flavius Josephus, Whiston translation, pg. 597).

Montanus:

"Likewise "Montanus"/Arrius Piso (the mountain) "is spared out of consideration for his father" when Thrasea Paetus is killed." Ref. "The True Authorship of the New Testament," in "The Proof that Josephus as Calpurnius Piso," pg. 20, Abelard Reuchlin, 1979, 1986. Note that this is found in the Annals of Tacitus, XVI, 33, Loeb. "Montanus" is found in "People in Pliny", Ronald Syme, JRS, 1968-69, pg. 149-150. And in Tacitus, Histories, III, 35. 2; and in Tacitus, Annals, Book XVI, XXIX, pg. 381, Loeb. Tacitus, Annals, Book XVI, XXXIII, pg. 387, Loeb. "Montanus" is mentioned in Juvenal, IV. 107, 131, Loeb.

Arrius Antoninus:

Arrius Antoninus was proconsul under Vespasian in 69 CE (Ref. "The Consulate of the Elder Trajan", by John Morris, JRS, Vol. 43-45, 1953-1955, pg. 79-80. And Josephus, BF, 4, 9, 2 (499); Tacitus, Histories, II, I, cf. 1, 10; Suetonius, 'The Twelve Caesars', under "Titus", 5. He is also in the Historia Augusta by this name. He is grandfather of emperor Antoninus Pius. And we have found that Antoninus Pius and Suetonius were one and the same (Ref. Antoninus Pius, 1, 4; and "The True Authorship of the New Testament," Abelard Reuchlin. Also see 'Marcus Aurelius' (A Biography), Appendix 2, 'The Antonine Dynasty', B: Antoninus Pius, pg. 242, Birley, published by Yale University Press, c. 1986.

Annius Varus:

In the Historia Augusta, Annius Verus is given as the great-grandfather of Marcus Aurelius (Ref. Marcus Aurelius, 1. 4). This "Annius Varus" (Arrius Piso) was obviously the founder of the "Annii Verii" (i.e., the

Antonine Dynasty). You will find quite a bit of information regarding this family and the names that they used in the work titled 'Marcus Aurelius' (A Biography), Appendix 2, 'The Antonine Dynasty', C: ANNII VERII (pg. 243-244), by Birley, pub. by Yale Univ., c. 1986. Arrius is "M. Annius Verus" (even dared to give us the "M" for "Marcus in Marcus Antonius!), suff. in 97 (Ref. "People in Pliny", Ronald Syme, JRS, 1968-1969, pg. 137).

Annius Gallus:

"Annius Gallus" is in Plutarch's "Lives" under "Otho". And Juvenal also makes mention of a "Gallus" in his works (Juvenal, VII. 144, Loeb). Tacitus, II, Histories, Book II, XLIV, pg. 233; and Tacitus, II, Histories, Book II, XXXIII, pg. 215; as well as Tacitus, II, Histories, Book II, XI; and Tacitus, II, Histories, Book I, LXXXVII, pg. 151.

Cestius Gallus and Gessius Florus:

The Roman writer Martial mentions Cestius Gallus in his works (Ref. Martial, XLII, 2.,Loeb). Josephus speaking about Gessius Florus (i.e., himself as Roman General and procurator of Judea says; "… nor could anyone out do him in disguising the truth." He is right about that, he is the all-time champion at disguising the truth! Ref. Josephus, pg. 484, Whiston. Also note that as "Gessius", Arrius could pronounce his alias name as "Jes(I)us." And in the royal language he could change vowels to render "Josi(ph)us" or simply "Jos" as short for "Josephus".

Antonius Primus:

Antonius Primus is found described in Tacitus, Histories, Book II, LXXXVI, pg. 299. In the works of Flavius Josephus, "Antonius Primus" turns into "Antonius Julianus."

Church father Origen says that to find out about the destruction of the Temple look in (the works of) Flavius Josephus and "Antonius Julianus" as if Antonius Julianus was a contemporary historian with Flavius Josephus and well-known. But there wasn't any historian known as "Antonius Julianus" except for being another name or alias of Arrius Piso!

One may note that the name "Antonius Julianus" is in the works of Flavius Josephus, but that is just another alias name that is used by Arrius Piso. Josephus calls himself "Joseph" (as in the father of Jesus), on pg. 427 of the works of Flavius Josephus, Whiston. There is a joke/allusion to Josephus being Arrius Piso by use of a reference to a passage in the works of Flavius Josephus which appears in the New Testament as given by Julius Piso in the Revelations. It is the "I am Alpha and Omega, the beginning and the end." The name "Arrius Piso" starts with "A" (Alpha) and ends with "O" (Omega). Julius refers to a statement that may be found on pg. 427 of the works of Flavius Josephus, Whiston. Ref. Rev. 1:8, 11; 21:6; 22:13.

And here is a great piece of rhetoric in the works of Flavius Josephus; "...and where it must be reproachful to write lies, when they must be known by the reader to be such." Note that he says "known by the READER," not the writer!!! (pg. 428, Josephus, Whiston). Like Alexander (the brother of Aristobulus), Arrius Piso "composed four books against his enemies." Those, of course, are the "Gospels." This is what we know of as and call "propaganda", and this was used during the 'war' as a part of the tactics against their enemies. So, when it is said that the New Testament was written as a part of the war, this is what is meant. Arrius Piso, writing as "Flavius Josephus" was here alluding to what he did by writing the Gospels (Ref. Flavius Josephus, pg. 458, Whiston).

"...and by degrees he laid blame on these men (his enemies) whose names were in these books, ..." Again, alluding to what he did. And we have found that this is true. He does place 'blame' on the Jews for the death of Jesus in his story and he does get more and more anti-Semitic in the Gospels as each one was written. Another thing is that he does place them in his works by their real names and by alias names with their 'profiles' so that people who knew these persons with a great familiarity would know of whom he was referring to (Ref. Flavius Josephus, pg. 459, Whiston).

Here is an admission to what he was doing; "yet were there fictitious stories added to what was really done." Ref. Josephus, pg. 517, Whiston. And about the 'signs' that the Temple and Jerusalem would be destroyed, he says;"... the signs were so evident..." and that "... (the Jews) did not regard the denunciations that God made to them. ["God" in this case being Arrius Piso himself] Thus, there was a star resembling a sword [he is referring to his 'sword', i.e. "Jesus" which was his strength as the bright morning star, like Achilles had with his "evening star"], which stood over the city (of Jerusalem), that continued (lasted) for a whole year." There at the end he could be referring to his position as Roman procurator in Judea.

Josephus/Arrius Piso states further... "I suppose the account of it would seem to be a fable, ..." Ref. Flavius Josephus, pg. 582, Whiston.

And "… as if they had been ready to (play as)/be "actors" against them." Ref. Flavius Josephus, pg. 602, Whiston.

"Some of them be took themselves to the writing of fabulous narrations…" Ref. Flavius Josephus, pg. 608, in "Against Apion", Whiston.

"As for myself, I have composed a true history of that whole war…" Josephus calls it a "war", not a "revolt" as most others do. He says; "I "acted" as general…" Ref. Flavius Josephus, pg. 609, in "Against Apion", Whiston.

Josephus the Actor… He says; "…and as for the History of the War, I wrote it as having been an "actor" myself…" Ref. Flavius Josephus, pg. 610, in "Against Apion," Whiston.

"I say nothing of such kings as have been famous for piety, particularly of one of them whose name was Cresus,…" "Cresus" is part "C(h)r(ist)" and part "(J)esus"… what a joker! Ref. Flavius Josephus, pg. 628, in "Against Apion," Whiston translation.

CHAPTER II:

THE IRREVERENT ELEMENT

ROMAN SEXUAL ATTITUDES & CHRISTIANITY

Writing about Roman life as evidenced in the sexual theme of archaeological finds that have been amassed from all parts of what once was the Roman Empire, including the cities that were buried by the eruption of Mount Vesuvius in the year 79 C.E. (A.D.), Joseph Jay Deiss* reminds us that at the time in which the New Testament was being written sex was a large part of the Roman humor and items with explicit sexual themes were common in day to day life.

He says, "Prostitution was certainly openly practiced, as it was not illegal. Sexual attitudes frequently reveal themselves in the painting and statuary favored by their owners. Nudity was not shocking." And he says," Their point of view was one of easy-going naturalism. The erect phallus was (seen as) a potent charm, and it appeared and reappeared everywhere: on shop signs, on equipment, on jewelry, in paintings, and on statues." So, is it really that surprising to find that same theme running through, being hinted at and used as the center of thinly veiled jokes in the literature of the time? Well, examples of that have long been known to scholars. These are especially found within the works of the poets of the time, but elsewhere as well.

Deiss says, "All living things (depicted), even the spout of a fountain (as a phallus) , respond in kind, for this was all a (running) joke." So, how is it that we should not expect to find this very same theme as a running joke in literature as well? Pliny the Younger hinted at this when he said, "In literature, as in life..." (Loeb Classical Library Edition, Book II, pg. 65).

And, how better to "increase the effect" as Pliny seems to have indicated several times, than to place those sexually oriented jokes within texts where the contrast would be the greatest? Now, where might that be? In the New Testament, of course!

Most people today have no idea of how life actually was then as compared to life as we are used to it today. And this really is a shame, as this is actually so much more important than the populace have ever begun to realize. In those times, as was just shown above, sex was a main theme of humor and to maximize its effect, what better way than to insert it, in disguised form, into what most people would then begin to consider sacred and holy? To the Roman authors, that would be the ultimate joke!

What better way and place to brag about misdeeds and crimes than in a place that people would never think of looking for them? And knowing full well that they could say and confess anything at all, and never be held accountable or punished for it – because it would not be discovered until after they had long since departed life!

* "Herculaneum: Italy's Buried Treasure," Joseph Jay Deiss, 1985, Harper & Row, New York.

THE TRUE SEXUAL NATURE OF THE NEW TESTAMENT TEXTS

There are sexually perverted themes that are found all throughout the New Testament texts, many of them involve the sexual abuse of women and children. Below are compiled examples of these and explanation of the true meaning of the words and phrases in those passages. (From the actual earliest known Greek texts of the New Testament, keyed to "The Greek/English Interlinear New Testament" by George R. Berry)

THE BOOK OF MARK

Mark 2:12 is a sexual joke, "he arose, took up his bed and went (walking)..." The imagery, when one understands what "he arose" really means makes the joke work because he "got an erection, took up his bed (to use it for sexual activity) and went... (walking)." That he is not sad in this joke, but rather in a "happy" condition, which adds to the humor of the joke because one may envision the subject of the sentence walking, head held high, with an erection, carrying his bed (for use at any opportune moment).

But as we will soon discover, the words "walk" and "walking," even if they are merely inferred, have an alternate meaning that creates a whole different meaning in various places within the New Testament. By the way, this same joke is repeated in Luke 18:15-17, and John 5:8. Because some scholars were able to see these rude sexual jokes in the New Testament, they understood that the New Testament was created by the people who were famous for making these same kind of rude and crude sexual jokes – the Romans.

Mark 6:33, "many (knew) him." This was written when "knew," "know," and "knowing" meant that someone was having sex with them. And there certainly was a lot of "knowing" going on in the New Testament!

Mark 7:30, "and her daughter laid upon the bed..." This is one of those statements that is deliberately there to tempt people into having sexual thoughts. And we have to place this into the context of that time with all of the sex fests (fetes) that they had in the Roman Empire every month. Those were called 'fetes' and there was one each month of the year. It was a time when "every bond was loosed." When members of the same family were out in the open having sexual encounters with each other, and apparently children were allowed to watch and/or participate as there were no laws forbidding it. So you can see, once you understand how sexual the lives of Romans were and, how any mention of anything that had a possible sexual meaning was fodder for sexual thought. This is what is called by hypnotists as "suggestion," it is what makes hypnotism possible and what makes people act upon the urges that accompany such thoughts. Which, is just what the Church wanted as we shall see as we read on.

Mark 8:18, "having eyes, see ye not?" This has to do with the alternate meaning that the word "eyes" relate. An explanation on just how these Roman writers had created an entire INSIDE language that only the royals could understand, which ran parallel to what they were writing on the surface of their works which were to be read to and by those who were "commoners." You will find the explanation for how it is that we can determine the alternate usage of these key words at the end of this listing (after the passages from The Revelation).

Mark 8:25, "he put (his) hands again upon his eyes..." Here one will have to know that "hands" is synonymous with the male sex organs. Yes, this may sound very strange when one is first told of this, but it is something that has been noted by scholars before. And about the word for "eyes," it is spelled virtually the same as the word for "anus"; and so, the two are seen by those who were writing these passages as also the same.

So, the joke becomes obvious to those who know what the actual meaning that those words convey. So now we read in the above passages, "having (a couple of) anuses, you cannot see?" No, because you do not see with your anus! And, "he put his male sex organs again upon his anuses." We are talking about people who owned slaves and used them sexually. So, this is obviously a joke about them using their slaves in this way for sex.

Mark 9:33-37 is about the gang rape of a child. About passing around a child for sexual purposes. You may not be able to gather this in most English translations of this passage. Again, this is what a scholar may see when reading the text as it was originally written - in Koine Greek.

Mark 10:15, "...whoever shall not receive the kingdom of God as a little child, in no wise shall enter into it." This passage actually reads as, "whoever shall not receive the kingdom of God (i.e. royal privileges) as (concerns) a little child, in no way shall enter into IT." The "IT" in the passage does not refer to the kingdom of God (royalty), but "a little child." Yes, "enter into IT, the little child," in a sexual way. And so, this is about an orgy with children.

Mark 12:11, "isn't it marvelous in our eyes?!" This is the same as Matt. 21:42. The "it" in the sentence is a phallus as that is what goes into an "eye" (anus) in the homosexual sex act being described.

Mark 13:12, "children will rise up against parents, and (parents) will put to death them (the children)." It does not say that these are THEIR parents. It just says "parents." Which is another way of saying that people who are parents, i.e. "older" (who had children of their own). The authors are describing themselves.

And "children will rise up," means children with erections will put those erections up against people who are parents, and those people who are parents will put them to death. And why would they put those children to death? So that there will be no witnesses to that perversion. Perhaps this is why Arrius Piso was never caught and charged for his sexual perversions as Pliny the Younger was.

THE BOOK OF MATTHEW

James Ballantyne Hannay ("The Rise, Decline and Fall of The Roman Religion") understood the true nature of the Bible and wrote about how certain words had duel meanings. He wrote, for example, that the word "stones" in places used in the Bible was actually a euphemism for testes. As he knew, and others are learning today, the true nature of the Bible is sexual. You have already become educated to the truth about God being a created concept, but "God" was also used as a title that was inherited by successive royals. And so when you read "God" and it says something like that which is found in Matt. 3:9, "God" is being used as a title for a person who is playing "God" in that instance.

Matt. 3:9, "For I say to you that God is able from these stones (testes) to raise up children..." There is a duel meaning in this passage, but the one that we are looking at is that the person who is playing God in this passage is saying that his "stones" are able to "raise up children." In other words, he is saying that his testes can get children sexually aroused.

Matt. 5:38, "an eye for an eye..." Which really meant an "anus" for an "anus"... i.e. "you can do mine, if I can do yours." And remember that the spelling of these two words in the original Greek are very close in spelling so that a person who was fluent in Greek could get an idea of what was being said; if not on a conscious level, then on a subconscious level.

Matt. 7:3, "in thy brother's eye." Here we have the "eye" reference being used, but in addition to that we have the word "brother." Why is that? Because one who knows Roman history also knows, that back in that time the word "brother" has the double or alternate meaning of "male sexual partner." So now we read the sentence as, "in your male sex partner's anus!" Such is the construction of many, many of the New Testament passages. And continuing in Matt. 7:3, "consider not the beam... in thine own eye." Which is a crude joke meaning "Never mind that there is a huge 'beam'... in your anus."

Matt. 7:4, "Let me pull... the mote out of thine eye..." Also, "and, behold!, a beam (is) in thine own eye!"

Mat. 7:5, "... the beam OUT OF thine own eye." And, "the mote out of thy brother's eye!"

Matt. 9:29 "then he touched their eyes..." 9:30, "their eyes were opened..."

Matt. 10:21, "... and children will rise up against parents, and will put to death them (the children). As in Mark, this passage is the same. The older people who are parents themselves get the children to "rise up" and then they put them to death, so that there are no witnesses.

Matt. 18:1-6. In this passage a child is called "it." (18:2). And the word "heavens" means that he intends to use the child sexually, and then kill "it." But this was likely not unique to the royals of the time when Christianity was being created. Perhaps this was a practice of at least certain royals going back much further, and this is because of a pattern that can be seen in the practice of "sacrificing" children and virgins to "God."

Matt. 19:13-15, "Then were brought to him (Jesus) little children, that hands he might lay on them, and might pray; but the disciples rebuked them. But Jesus said, suffer the little children, and not forbid them to come to me; for of such is the kingdom of the heavens. And having laid upon them... hands, he departed then."

There are several things that one will notice about this statement. For one thing, it never says that he was laying hands on them to cure or heal them of anything or that they were cured of anything. It does say that he "touched" them and the passage could read that he "laid upon them." Also, "hands" is another sexual word that refers to male sex organs. Ballantyne had written about that in the work which had already been mentioned.

And, in our research on the subject of the sexual nature of the Bible we had already discussed what prayer really was/is. It is a mocking of someone giving oral sex. And so, that is also what it is used for as a euphemism in the Bible. So, given that information, what do you think that the passage above REALLY refers to?

The passage also gives the reader the impression that the disciples rebuked those who had brought the children to Jesus. But that is not the case. In fact, the people who brought the children, if the story had been true, would probably have been hired and paid to round up the children. Instead, reading the passage as we now know it, the "disciples," or those who were with "Jesus"/Arrius Calpurnius Piso, rebuked the children. In other words, they were harsh and mishandling them when "Jesus" spoke up and made it clear to them that those children were going to die, so that they did not need to get the children upset or slap them around - unless they wanted to.

Jesus/Arrius Piso says in the passage as if addressing the parents of the children, "suffer" because the little children have come to him (to be used sexually and then to be killed), but do not forbid them to come to him, because that is his privilege as a royal.

And then he says in Matt. 19:17, "Why do you call me good? No one is good..." He (Arrius Piso) is mocking the fact that he has fooled so many people into believing that he, as Jesus, is "good."

Matt. 20:33, "Lord, that our eyes may be opened..."

Matt. 21:42 "Isn't it marvelous in our EYES?!" The word "it" being the operative word in connection to the word "eyes." "It," of course, is a phallus.

THE BOOK OF LUKE

As with anything that is just learned and new to a person, this may take a few readings to fully absorb. It would take time and space in this book to explain in great detail each and every passage herein and so one will have to learn the key words and then read the sentences and phrases that have not been fully explained.

Luke 6:20 "And he lifted up his eyes on this disciple..." He (Arrius Piso/Jesus) let his friends have use of his male sex slaves by having them, while in a kneeling position, present their rear quarters for ready entry.

Luke 6:41 "beholdest... the mote... in thy brother's eye..."

Luke 9:47-48, "... having taken ahold of a little child he (Jesus) set IT by him, and said unto them (who were with him), whoever shall receive (take and sexually abuse) this little child in my name (meaning by his power and authority as a royal), receives (the benefit of the power of) me (that is mine). For he who is less among you all, he shall be great." He who is "less" is less for having ejaculated. So, the true meaning of the statement is as if it was a game or a contest to see who would be the winner for having had sex the most, and therefore, having ejaculated the most. You will find that this is a re-occurring theme throughout the New Testament. The "goal" as defined by the authors is to achieve orgasm in their various sexually perverted escapades as they have documented them within the New Testament texts.

Luke 11:7 "cause me no trouble, the door has already been shut (for privacy), and my children are (now) with me in bed; I cannot rise up (get an erection) to give (it) to thee." In other words, he is busy having sex with his children and does not want to be bothered with an invitation for sex with someone else. So, here we have an example of incest in the New Testament.

Luke 17:34 "(and) there shall be two men in one bed..." Really, a lot of this is actually a "no-brainer" as the meanings are so obvious. They wrote what they did, as they did for specific reasons. There is a subconscious or subliminal message in this sentence that the foremind may not pick up. In reading the sentence your attention is drawn to the word "bed." However, the mind breaks things down and reads this as well, "there shall be two men in one" ("...there shall be two men in one [in] bed"). Which is a homosexual threesome, an act of oral and anal sex performed upon one man by two other men. Or, simply as "two men in one bed" as two men engaging in sex with each other in a bed.

Luke 18:15-17 (is the same as Mark 2:12 and John 5:8).

Luke 24:31 "Their eyes were opened, and they knew..." As our research has revealed "eye" is synonymous with "anus." And to "know" or having "known" someone, means having sex with them. So, how do we read this? "Their anus was opened (for each other), and they fornicated."

THE BOOK OF JOHN

There is actually much more to the Gospel of John that could be covered here. But, that really isn't the reason for this listing. So, let's cover this later in more detail. The purpose, once again, of listing all of these instances that occur within the New Testament texts is to provide the reader with the information necessary for being able to see and understand the true sexual nature of the texts and to prove that this theme is consistent throughout all of the New Testament material.

John 1:1 "the word." The "word" ("logos") is God, and the Christian God is the phallus. As this becomes obvious in the various statements that revolve around the phallus. Oh, another thing that we have learned is that there is usually more than one or two meanings for each of the words, phrases and sentences that the authors had composed. And in order to keep track of and understand these, one will have to build a file of cross-referenced material. This phrase, for instance, relates to others which are found elsewhere. When these are seen together, the meaning becomes clear.

John 4:22 is both a disclaimer and a declaration, and it hints at what we have already discovered, "you worship you know not what." That "what" is sexual perversion as represented in the form of the phallus. That is, depravity and the phallic god of lust.

John 4:35 "Lift up your eyes... (and prepare to be...)" Knowing the meaning of the word "eyes" you can figure out what this means. It was already explained earlier.

John 5:8 "Rise, take up your bed, and walk." This is the same joke that was explained when we had examined Mark 2:12 and Luke 18:15-17.

John 6:5 "when Jesus/Arrius Piso then lifted up (his lifted thing) [to the]... eyes,..." He, Arrius Piso, had his sex slaves position themselves; most likely in a row to be mounted by him and his friends, with their behinds up, offering easier access.

John 8:44 "the lusts of your father you will do (with him)." This is a phrase that no doubt was used to convince children to submit to incest with their parents. There are many such passages throughout the

New Testament. Remember, they were put there on purpose and were deliberately crafted as we have found them to be.

John 9:6 "he (Jesus) spat on the ground, and made clay of his spittle...," "and he anointed the eyes... with the clay." Well, "spat" could mean ejaculate. And he may have used something mixed with it to make a 'salve' of some kind. Remembering that we DO know the meaning of some of the words in this sentence, we are then able to deduce what the rest of it may mean. For example, knowing their crude form of sexual humor, it is not hard to imagine them joking about the word 'spat' as meaning ejaculation. And when one of them were to ejaculate on the ground, turning that into a joke about them having made "clay."

John 9:10 "How were thine eyes opened?"

John 9:11 "A man called Jesus made clay... and anointed mine eyes..." This shows us the true meaning in Genesis where it says that God made man out of the earth. "Clay" or "earth" (life) with "spittle" is a euphemism for semen.

John 21:5 "Then Jesus therefore says to them, "little children, have you any food?" This is a very dirty statement knowing the true sexual nature of the New Testament texts. He (Arrius Piso), lets those who are privy to his meaning imagine what kind of sexual "food" he could be giving to the little children. For those who wonder, he answers thus saying in the following verses that this "food" is "fishes." Our research has already revealed that "fish" or "fishes" refer to sex organ/s; in this instance, the male sex organ/s. So now the privy reader may understand what his statement actually means.

ACTS (OF THE APOSTLES)

The Acts of the Apostles is full of filthy sex commentary and in fact the travels of "Paul" in the Acts are really there as an advertisement for the most popular brothels in the Roman Empire, placed there to inform all readers where the places were located – so that the people who they were tempting could travel to them for "sex" vacations. That this is so should be obvious to anyone who has seriously studied the New Testament.

Acts 5:6 "young men arose..." "Young men," that is to say young teenaged boys (like altar boys), and we know what "arose" means (they got an erection).

Acts 9:30 "When the brethren knew..." The brethren (male sex partners) "knew," i.e. "fornicated."

Acts 9:34 "maketh thee (a youth) whole (become a "man" by deflowering), arise! (get your erection and get used to it)."

Acts 20:12 "brought the young man "alive"..." "Alive" means "erect." In other words, an "alive" phallus.

THE BOOK OF ROMANS

The first chapter of Romans is about homosexuality.

Romans 1:26-27 "For this reason God gave them up to passions of dishonor, for both their females changed the natural use into that contrary to nature; and in like manner also the males having left the natural use of the female, were inflamed in their lust toward one another, males with males, working out shame, and the recompense which was fit of their error in themselves (were they) receiving." The God of the New Testament was the phallus. But at the same time, it was also a title that was held by Arrius Piso, and his little invention, "Jesus."

Romans 7:1 "Know ye not brethren?" The meaning of which we have already seen used elsewhere. The key words here are "know" and "brethren." So, it reads, "(Do) you fornicate not, (my) male sexual partners?"

Romans 8:22 "We know (so) that the whole of creation groans." It says, "We fornicate so that the whole Church (their invention) groans." They are saying that in all of the early Christian Churches there is so much fornicating going on that one can hear the moans and groans within the churches very clearly.

Romans 9:21 "Hath not the potter power over the clay?" The potter is the maker of "vessels" and vessels are human beings, and "clay" (semen) makes the vessels (human beings). So, this is secretly saying "Does not a man have power over his own semen?"

THE BOOK OF I CORINTHIANS

I Cor. 1:9-10 "Whatsoever the God (the new Christian God, "Jesus"/ Arrius Piso) prepared for those of us who love (fornicated with) him, but to us the God (Arrius Piso) revealed..."

This means that Arrius Piso, who invented and played both God and Jesus in the Gospels had sex with those whom he was close to; perhaps inferring incest. But also now knowing that Arrius Piso himself, like Pliny the Younger, had homosexual sex – we now know that the "donkey" that the Talmud says that Pliny (in the Talmud pronounced "ploy-nee al-moy nee") fornicated with, was Arrius Piso!

I Cor. 3:3 "... for yet, fleshy ye are..." "are ye not fleshy, and walk according to (the lusts) of men?" "fleshy" refers to the "fleshy" part of a man, the part that can be grabbed and squeezed; the sex organs. So read, "are you not fleshy (down there), and "walk" (use your "feet," i.e. sex organs) like other men?" Both hands and feet are used as euphemisms for male sex organs. And to "walk" or "walking" is to make use of the feet. In other words, "walk" means "fornicate."

I Cor. 3:6 "I planted (the sex member), Apollos "watered" (ejaculated); but the God (Arrius Piso) gave growth (erected his sex organ)."

I Cor. 5:7-8 This talks about "The Lump" and unleavened bread – which we have already discussed when we had examined the sick and dirty jokes in the New Testament. And so, we know that this refers to bread that was made out of or by mixing in human dung.

I Cor. 6:16 "Or know ye not (?)" This was something that became an insider's catch phrase. Something that could be said quickly to another person. As a bit of humor, one priest might pass another and say, "know ye not?" And they both would know what that meant and laugh to themselves about it. "... that he that is joined (in the sex act) to the whore is (like) one body? For shall (there) be, he says, the two for one (intertwined in) flesh (deal)." This could be a reminder to some of a promotional deal for the great Roman brothels (Church or otherwise) saying, "bring along a friend to try it out for free!" A "two for one" deal. Like we see in ads today for pizza and other things. Perhaps that to some may sound like a stretch now; but that is because those persons are still unaware of all of the instances that we have already found where little ads and promos have been placed within various texts from that time.

And don't forget that in the book 'The Synthesis Of Christianity' we had already discussed the fact that "Paul's" travels to the locations of the great Roman brothels were simply written as advertisement for those brothels. Throughout the whole New Testament there are titillating statements that were placed there deliberately by the authors to get the whole congregation hot and bothered so that the Church leaders could make their money from the sex trade right there in the little sex booths that were built into the Church walls!

I Cor. 7:9 "But if they have not self-control (and need to fornicate urgently and frequently), let them marry; for it is better to marry than to burn (in the loins)." Yes, people have thought that this meant "burn in hell." No, it meant that burning pressure and itch that males, particularly teenaged boys, have in their loins and also at the same time they meant that it is better to marry and be with one loyal woman than to visit the brothels and get a venereal disease and "burn in the loins." So, in that last sense, this was another of those "disclaimers" of which we have already found so many in the New Testament texts.

I Cor. 9:11 "(it is) a great thing if your fleshy things we shall reap?" You know what "fleshy things" are. The male sex organs. This appears to be an allusion to what the Romans did with the captured Jewish soldiers when the Jewish freedom fighters (Pharisees) were starving inside the city of Jerusalem; they cut off their male sex organs and flung them over the walls knowing that starvation would guarantee that they would be consumed by those who were starving inside.

I Cor. 10:7 "... the people sat down to eat, and to drink, and rose up to play." This is the source for "eat, drink, and be merry." To "eat" is to take into the mouth, the male sex organ (as we have already seen demonstrated earlier when "Jesus" asked the children if they were hungry), and to "drink" is to swallow the ejaculate. You should know what "rose up" means (erection); and to "play" is "fornicate." I Corinthians is so full of filthy statements that all of it, honestly, may never be exposed..

I Cor. 15:52 "... in an instant, in (the) twinkling of an eye, at the last trumpet; for a trumpet will sound, and the dead shall be raised (up) incorruptible, and we shall be changed." This is ALL "sex talk."

James B. Hannay was right, there IS "much in the Bible that is just too gross for translation." The "twinkling of an eye" is the muscle twitches of the anus with the male sex organ in it. And the "sound" of a trumpet is made because of the air that has been "pumped" into it (the anus) when the male sex member is removed from it. And the "dead" means the un-erect organ. So, the un-erect male sex organ/s "shall be raised" (become erect). Why incorruptible? Because they are ALREADY corrupt. And they are "changed" because they have had intercourse and have ejaculated.

II CORINTHIANS

II Cor. 1:9 "God who raises the dead." Not such a great trick now that we know what this really means.

II Cor. 1:11 "laboring together." Now this means having exhaustive, sweaty sex. The use of the words "labor" and "work" were indicators of how hard and intense they were busily having sexual incounters.

II Cor. 2:4 "... that the love ye might know which I have more abundantly towards you." The key words here are "love," "know" and "abundantly." "Abundantly" here means multiple sexual encounters with one person – the person who this is being addressed to. This recalls the use of the Roman word for abundant... "abondanza!"

II Cor. 2:6 "the greater part." We have found Pliny the Younger using this phrase in his epistles, apparently alluding to this and other passages that say the same thing. "The greater part" or "the better part" is the main male sex organ which is represented by the phallus. This phrase is used when Mary Magdalene is washing the feet of Jesus, and "Jesus" says to Martha that Mary has chosen "the better part." Thus, we have an example of *feet* being used as a euphemism for the male sex organ/s.

II Cor. 4:2 "... walking in craftiness..." This means that they (the authors) were "getting off" by thinking of how they have had "fornicated" the minds of those readers (and believers) of their "holy" texts. They had pulled off a massive hoax that they knew would last for hundreds or even thousands of years before it would be discovered. They were just ejaculating constantly at the thought of what they had done and how they would always be remembered for it. They were huge egotists.

II Cor. 5:2 "for indeed, in this we groan..." Yes, we know now how much they were moaning and groaning, but they had to just keep on "bragging" about it anyway. So, should we change "In God We Trust," to "In God We Moan and Groan"?

II Cor. 5:4 "that may be swallowed up..." An allusion to ejaculate being swallowed. Or anything else of a sexual nature that this may fit. It could be a sex organ being "swallowed up" by an orifice.

II Cor. 7:1 "we should cleanse ourselves from every defilement of the flesh..." This appears to refer to a requirement which was instituted at the brothels that the sex participants clean themselves after the sex act. Particularly the prostitutes themselves.

II Cor. 7:4 "I have been filled..." "I over abound..." This is the true meaning of "my cup runneth over." The word "cup" (for instance), means any sex orifice that can be used to hold semen. In this passage, "I have been filled" means that someone has ejaculated in someone's anus. And "I over abound..." means that it is spilling out of his orifice. Nice to think about young children reading this, isn't it?

II Cor. 7:5 "our flesh had not any ease..." No, not at all. Because they were "using" their "flesh" constantly.

II Cor. 8:24 "the proof therefore of your love..." The "proof" of their fornication is the orgasm, the ejaculate.

II Cor. 11:9 "for the deficiency of me the brethren completely filled up..." The void or empty space, in the orifice (whichever that may be) the male sex partner had completely filled up, with you-know-what.

THE BOOK OF EPHESIANS

So far, you have learned the actual meaning of several of the words that were used in the New Testament and how knowing those true meanings changes the whole meaning within the New Testament texts. But there are many other words of which you will learn the true or alternate meanings, and this will likewise change the meaning of many other passages. Such as the meaning of the word "spirit" (as horniness). When one realizes these things they can visualize just how these things were used as jokes in the everyday lives of priests and how many priests today still live this kind of secret life. For instance, if two priests were spying on a couple having a sexual encounter and the male is particularly zealous in the act, one might say to the other that "the boy certainly has spirit!" In other words, that is to say that he is a horny little bast***! Yes, such is the true nature of the New Testament and of religion in terms of those who are in the positions of authority. The leaders of the Church or religion in general are NOT "believers" – they never have been. That is the cold sober truth of the matter.

Eph. 4:3 "... bearing with one another (each other) in love (sex), being diligent (mindful) to keep the unity (connection) of the spirit (horniness) in the (sexual) bond of peace (sexual gratification)." Yes, that is correct.

Eph. 4:4 "(two people) [as] one body and one spirit (horniness)." Two horny people connected sexually in the horniness. I have no doubt that many of those who read about the passages will become... well, shall we say "aroused" at the thought of them. Which is proof of the power of suggestion, the suggestion that these passages were intended to "inspire."

Eph. 4:5 "... one baptism..." Baptism is the covering with "water." Which is the life-force, and for which is a euphemism for "semen" – the other liquid life-force. And covering someone with it is representative of "conquering" them. And "one" baptism puts it into perspective as representing the deflowering" of a person. So, "baptism" was used as a euphemism for being initiated into sexual activity. Again, we can just imagine how this might have been used in a joke by Popes and priests alike, as well as other Church authorities who were in on the jokes and understood the meaning of these words.

Eph. 4:8 "... ascended up high..." This is to say that a male sex member was erected up high.

Eph. 4:9 "... into the lower parts..." Or in other words, the prime sexual area of the body.

Eph. 4:10 "... that he might fill all (sexual) things..." In this case, the meaning is to ejaculate into all of the sex orifices.

Eph. 4:28 "... but rather let him labor, working with his own, what good (he does) with (his) hands, that he may have (sexual talent) to impart (share) with him that has need (of it)..." Again, "labor" means intense sexual activity, and "working" means fornicating. And you should know the rest of the meaning of this passage.

Eph. 4:29 "let not every corrupt word (logos = God = phallus) go forth out of your mouth..." Note that "corrupt" here means "loaded with" or full of semen. In other words, keep that phallus in your mouth and let it empty its "corruptness" inside the mouth.

Eph. 5:1-2 "be ye, therefore, imitators of God (the Christian God = Arrius Piso), as with children beloved (being fornicated with, abused) and walk (fornicate) in love (fornication)..." The phrase "walk in love" means "use the sexual organs in the act of fornication."

Eph. 5:14 "(be ye) aroused (thou) that sleepest, and rise up (become erect) from among the dead (the un-erect state), and shall (you see the) shine upon the (wet) Christ (phallus)."

Eph. 6:6 "... not (just) with eye-service as men-pleasers, but as bondsmen (being sexually bound) of the Christ (erect phallus)." What a totally different meaning all of this has when it is examined intelligently.

Remember that "eye" means 'anus.' And so, this is saying sexual "service" with the anus. And to make certain that the privy reader understands clearly that "eye" means anus, the writer of this line includes the phrase "men-pleasers" because men are the ones who use, and into which they specifically, put their prime male sex organs. And being "bound men of the phallus," is being sexually connected by the male sex organ while in the sex act. Now we have finally exposed those "dirty birds" and no one will be able to read these passages in the same way again.

THE BOOK OF GALATIANS

Gal. 1:1 "... Jesus Christ (Arrius Piso's name for his prime male sex member) and God the Father (the God-Father) who raised him (up) from (the) dead (state) and all the brethren with me..." By now, you should know how to read this fully.

Gal. 1:10 "do I seek men to please? For if yet men I were pleasing (with sex), Christ's bondsman I should not be." And what is the meaning of this statement? It is that the subject is not into pleasing other men, he is out to be pleased himself. And THAT is what makes him worthy of being bound to "Christ" (aka Arrius Piso) sexually. The underlying rule that we find here is that each person is expected to get their OWN "rocks off" and not worry about pleasing anyone else.

Gal. 1:16 "to reveal his son in me (sexually)" The "son" of God (Arrius Piso) is his "invention" Jesus; and this happens to also be what he called his prime sex member. And so, the author of this line is saying that Arrius Piso had his 'son' (little Jesus) in him, sexually. In other words, in his anus.

Gal. 2:9 "James and Cephas and John, those reputed to be pillars, right hands, they gave to me and Barnabas for fellowship..." First of all, the key words and phrases here are: "pillars," "right hands," and "fellowship." The word "pillar" is a euphemism for phallus. Right hands are the hands that most people use as most people are right-handed. And so, this is the hand that they also used when masturbating. They are also used to refer to the phallus as such, because of the sexual connection. Remember to read the sentence carefully. If they are pillars, and that means "phallus," and they are also "right hands" then that makes the phrase "right hands" synonymous with phallus also. This is what is called a precedent example. It is used to establish the alternate meaning of words or phrases. And "fellowship" is brethren "coming together." In other words, fornicating with each other. No doubt you have heard believers talk about fellowship or fellowshipping and 'they know not what they speak'!

Gal. 3:3 "now in the flesh (of the fleshy things) are ye being (made to) be (feel) better?" In other words, "now, in the act of sex doesn't your flesh (sex areas) feel better?" Or "doesn't sex feel good???"

Gal. 4:15 "having plucked yourself (your penis) out of eyes (anuses) ye had given them (the anuses) to me (to have my turn at to go into)." Remember, the authors of the New Testament knew very well what they were doing.

Yes, what a totally different meaning we find once we understand the true meaning of the words that they had used. And, also remember that these authors meant this meaning secretly, but on the surface many ignorant people took the passages literally and were mutilated either by themselves or others because of not being able to understand the true meanings.

Gal. 4:19 "my (little children), of whom I "labor" in..." Again, the word "labor" means intense fornication.

Gal. 5:13 "... for an occasion to the flesh (masturbation), but (instead) by love (sex) serve (service) ye one another." That is, instead of masturbating by yourself, you should be having sex with someone.

Gal. 5:14 "thou shalt love (fornicate with) thy neighbor as (by) thyself (you practice sex)." So, the "love thy neighbor" thing is really saying "get out there and fornicate!" Instead of masturbating.

Gal. 5:17 "For the flesh (fleshy things) desires against the spirit (i.e. sexual release as opposed to horniness), and the spirit (horniness) against the flesh (horniness begs release from the fleshy things), and these things are opposed to each other (horniness & release), that not whatsoever ye may wish those things (even if you don't wish horniness & release), ye should DO (you should do IT); but if by the spirit (the horniness) ye are led, ye are under no law (against it)." In other words, "so go for it!"

Gal. 5:22 "But the fruit (gain or semen) of the spirit (horniness) is love (sex), joy (sexual pleasure during the act), peace (sexual gratification, release, afterglow)..."

Gal. 6:5 "For each (man) shall bear (carry) his own "load" (of semen)." The word "load" as being synonymous with semen has been incorporated into many, many rude jokes and people have generally understood this meaning.

Gal. 6:11 "See how large (this papyrus roll of letters is that) I wrote (ejaculated) with my own hand!" Remember that anything that they saw that could be interpreted as phallic they most certainly made note of it and used as a euphemism. They wrote in the form of papyrus rolls, which were like rolled up sheets of paper that formed a long "tube," and so, of course that was compared to a phallus.

THE BOOK OF PHILIPPIANS

Phil. 1:2 "... peace (sexual gratification) from God (Arrius Piso) our father and the Lord (curious) Christ Jesus." There are many words in this passage that ALL mean "phallus." "God," "Father," "Lord," "Christ," and "Jesus." One who knows all about this can just see Arrius Piso making jokes by pointing towards his prime male member. Such as, "this is your Father!"

Phil. 1:9 "I pray (do oral sex) that your love (fornication or sex act) yet more and more may abound (increase to overflowing)..."

Phil. 1:11 "being filled with fruit (of the loins)..." Again, here we find "fruit" as semen.

Phil. 1:16 "to arouse (myself) to my (sexual) bonds (in flesh), but those (bonds around the fleshy things) out of love (fornication)..." Being "bound" or having "bonds" in these sexual terms means being tightly connected in the act of sex. In most instances that we find this in the New Testament, this is referring to a phallus (prime male member) being tightly held within an anus.

Phi. 1:18-19 "... I will rejoice (have repeated sexual pleasure)... for I "know" (fornicate)..."

Phil. 1:27 "... that ye stand fast in one spirit..." Means... that you stay hard in your erection and reach the approach of orgasm with both sex partners working for that same common goal of orgasm; "in one spirit," of course, meaning "in mutual horniness."

Phil. 2:2 "fulfill my joy..." Means "fulfill my sexual pleasure."

Phil. 2:13 "to work (fornicate) according to good (sexual) pleasure."

Phil. 2:16 "that not in vain I ran (quickly used my "feet") nor in vain "labored." He quickly used his prime male member and "labored" (fornicated), and it was NOT in vain. Meaning that he achieved climax (orgasm).

Phil. 2:29 "receive therefore him in the Lord (phallus) with all joy (sexual pleasure during the act)..." Oh, "joy!"

Phil. 3:13 "Brethren, I myself do not reckon to have laid the (fleshy) things behind (it) and to the (fleshy) things before (in front) [which is] stretching out (becoming erect) towards the goal (that) I pursue for the prize of the calling on high (the urging of the erection) of God (the phallus) in (the "spirit" of, i.e. "horniness of") Christ Jesus (the "phallus, phallus!")."

Phil. 3:16 "... by the same rule to walk (and) to be of the same mind." That is to "walk" (fornicate) with both parties being horny.

Phil. 3:17 "be imitators together of me brethren..." He is saying to "get together" and imitate him in his sex acts, male sex partners." Why? So as to learn what it is that "turns him on" and "gets him off." Because, "thus walking as you have, (there is) a pattern for us (to follow)." That is to say that, fornicating as you have, you will see a pattern as to what it takes for him to climax..

Phil. 3:18 "for many are walking..." Yes, in those days, many were "walking" (fornicating).

Phil. 4:1 "so that my brethren (who are) beloved and longed for, my joy and crown, thus stand fast in the Lord beloved." Oh, that sounds so sweet doesn't it? Here is what it really means... "brethren" (male sex partners) who are "beloved" (being fornicated with) and desired, his joy (sexual pleasure during the act) and his "crown" which is a euphemism for the "head" of his prime male sex organ. "stand fast" is to stay erect and fast in the sex act, and the phallus be fornicated (stimulated to orgasm)!

Phil. 4:3 "And the rest of my fellow-workers..." The rest of those with whom he fornicates.

Phil. 4:7 "... and the peace (sexual gratification) of God (the phallus)..."

Phil. 4:9 "... and the God of peace (the phallus of sexual gratification) shall be with you."

Phil. 4:12 "both to abound and to be deficient." That means to be full of semen and to be "spent" of it.

Phil. 4:17 "but I seek after (more) fruit that abounds on your account." He seeks after more semen that there is plenty of because of a certain person.

Phil. 4:18 "But I have all (fleshy) things and abound; I am full..." He has all of those male "fleshy things" and in abundance, he is full (of semen).

Phil. 4:19 "that but my (phallic) God will fill up all your need... (for semen)." And also knowing this, it kind of gives another meaning to the phrase, "let the (life) force be with you!"

THE BOOK OF COLOSSIANS

Col. 1:9 "that you may be filled..." Yes, "filled" with WHAT? That's the question.

Col. 1:9-10 "... and spiritual understanding for you to walk worthyly of the Lord to all the pleasure in every good work bringing forth fruit..." Okay, well, we know what "spiritual" really means (horniness), and we know what "walk" really means, "fornicating." So, "horny fornicating" worthy of the Lord (phallus) to the point of "all pleasure" during the sex act, "good work" is good fornicating, so as to bring forth the "fruit" (semen).

Col. 3:5 "Put to death therefore the (fleshy) members..." Meaning, take the "fleshy members" (prime male sex organs) to orgasm and let them "die" (un-erect).

Col. 3:7 "Among whom ye also walked once when ye were living in these (fleshy) things." Or, "Among whom you also fornicated with once when you were erect in these fleshy things (sexual male members)."

Col. 3:12 "... of God, holy, and beloved, bowels of compassion..." God in the New Testament is Arrius Piso, and "holy" means "sacred" and sacred in turn means "secret." "Beloved" is the act of being fornicated, and "bowels of compassion" means feeling (the prime male member) very deeply in the anus.

Col. 3:14-15 "And to all (of) these, increase love which is the bond of perfectness and the peace of the Christ (who is) God..." Increase fornication which is the bond (tight sexual connection) of perfection (the pleasure during the act of sexual intercourse) and the peace (the sexual gratification) of the Christ (phallus) who is (the Christian) God (Arrius Calpurnius Piso).

Col. 3:20 "Children, obey the parents (of children) [i.e. adults] in all (fleshy) things; for this is very pleasing (to) the Lord (Jesus)." This is advising children to do whatever adults may tell them to do with regards to sex. To obey them, no matter what, as this is what the Lord (Jesus, the big phallus) wants them to do.

Col. 3:22 "Bondsmen (slaves, sex slaves) obey all (sexual) things the masters (demand) according to the flesh (fleshy things, sexual things), not (merely) with eye-service (anal servicing) (and) as men-pleasers, but in (being silent about it) simplicity of heart (emotional essence), fearing the Lord (phallus) God (Arrius Piso)."

THE BOOK OF I THESSALONIANS

I Thes. 1:1 "whom he raised (made erect) from among the dead (un-erect prime male members)..."

I Thes. 2:7 "a nurse-maid (nursing maiden, lactating woman) would cherish her own children (share her lactation with her own children)." The inference is *at any age*. In other words, this is an incestuous statement.

I Thes. 2:9 "For ye remember brethren our labor and the toil for night and day working, for not to burden any one of you." Here, "brethren" is male sex partners, and "labor" is sweaty sex, and they were "toiling" at it night and day so that none of them will have that terrible burden of carrying their heavy "loads" around in their "fleshy things."

I Thes. 2:12 "for you to have walked worthily of God..." Is, "for you to have fornicated worthily of (the phallus) God..."

I Thes. 2:19 "for what (IS) our hope or joy or crown of boasting?" The hope is FALSE HOPE, their "joy" is the pleasure during the sex act, and the "crown" that they are boasting about is the head of the phallus – which is the theme and basis for the whole New Testament!

I Thes. 3:5 "Because of this, I also no longer (was) enduring, (and was) sent for to know your faith, lest perhaps he who tempts did tempt you, and void should become our labor." No longer "enduring" the pressure in his loins, and sent for to "know" your faith. This is "knowing WHILE having "faith." That is, having sex while having "faith" because "faith" means concentrating or focusing upon the sex act during the act. One can visualize that if one of the customers of the Church brothels was taking too long, a priest might come by and rap on the door saying "have faith!" Meaning focus on what you are doing and get finished. And "lest perhaps he who tempts you (the author of these titillating texts) tempts you to masturbate and make their labors (literary sex-work) to get them to come into the brothels void." Remember, they did not want anyone to masturbate and "get off" without paying for it. You can see their urgings for people to seek sex partners all through these texts.

I Thes. 3:8 "because now we live (are erect) if you stand fast in Lord." Yes, "stand fast in phallus!" Hard and fast in phallus!

I Thes. 4:9 "Now concerning brotherly love, ye have no need (for me) to write to you (about this), for you yourselves are taught of God (phallus) for to love (fornicate with) one another." As you should know by now "brotherly love" is fornicating with a male sex partner.

I Thes. 4:11 "and endeavor earnestly to be quiet (in your passions) and to do your own (fleshy) things, and to work with your own hands, even as (if) upon you we (are) enjoined, for ye may walk..." This is not advocating masturbation as it might appear as "work" is fornicate and "your own hands" does not mean "hands," but "male sex members." He goes on to say "even as if they are "enjoined" and fornicating. So, it is saying "do it" with someone else when he is not there to "do it" with. This is the earlier form of the sixties saying, "if you can't be with the one you want, then love the one you are with."

I Thes. 4:16 "and the dead (un-erect) in Christ (phallus) shall rise (erect) first (fast/quickly)..."

I Thes. 5:12 "But we beseech you brethren, to KNOW those who labor with you...." Yes, what a joke. Fornicate with those who you are having sweaty sex! As if they aren't already!

I Thes. 5:16-17 "always rejoice; unceasingly pray." This is saying always continue to experience the "joy" (pleasure during the sex act), and to never stop giving oral sex. (praying = oral sex on the phallus)

I Thes. 5:26 "Salute all the brethren with a holy kiss." First of all, "salute" is phallic. It is a "hand" going UP; which is to say an erect phallus. The "brethren" you already know is "male sex partners," and a "holy kiss" means a "secret kiss." Given all that we now know about this, would be cause to think that this is another name for male oral sex. Think of a big, fat, sloppy "kiss" placed just so, you-know-where. Doesn't that make sense?

THE BOOK OF II THESSALONIANS

II Thes. 1:2 "... peace (sexual gratification) [to you] from the God-Father and Lord Jesus Christ (phallus, phallus, phallus!)."

II Thes. 1:3 "Brethren..." (male sex partners) "... and the love (fornication) abounds of each one of you all to one another..." Yes, just one big orgy of sex.

II Thes. 1:11 "... and may fulfill every good pleasure (sexual pleasure during the act of having sex) of (the best) goodness (sexual pleasure of the best kind) and work of faith..." The fornication of faith, is the fulfillment of the act of sex, which is the climax or orgasm.

II Thes. 2:10 "... because (of) the love (fornication) of the truth..." That is to say that they totally "F'd" with the truth in their writings.

II Thes. 2:17 "... in every good word and work." In every "good" phallus, and a "good" phallus is an erect one. And "work," you know is "fornicate." So, in every "good" hard phallus, there is good fornicating.

II Thes. 3:1 "For the rest, pray, brethren, for us, that the word (logos = phallus) of the Lord (curious, phallus) may run..." And, "pray brethren" means oral sex with male sex partners. And the phallus of the bigger phallus may "run" instead of "walk." That he may reach an extra fast orgasm.

II Thes. 3:6 "... you withdraw from every brother walking disorderly..." This is withdrawing the "you-know-what" from the male sex partner, fornicating sloppily. Perhaps coming out during the course of the sex act because of the lack of "faith" (concentration).

II Thes. 3:8-9 "but in labor and toil, night and day working, for not to (let it) be burdensome to any one of you. Not that we have any authority, but that (as) ourselves, a pattern (of example) we might give to you for (you) to imitate us." Well, since this echoes something that we had already covered earlier so let's leave it at that.

II Thes. 3:10 "... that if anyone does not wish to work, neither let him eat (of the fleshy things)." No fornication, no phallus or semen in your mouth.

II Thes. 3:11 "Some are walking with you disorderly..." This has been taken to mean that they were getting drunk, but that was a cover for the actual meaning – to hide the sexual nature of the statement from those who have eyes and minds which are not privy to the true nature of these texts. "Walking disorderly," simply means "fornicating sloppily."

THE BOOK OF I TIMOTHY

I Tim. 1:19 "as to faith made shipwreck..." These were all crude sex jokes. "shipwreck" is a euphemism for a phallus which has just been "spent" and lay wet upon the sexual partner. It is no longer in the "water" floating around; it is washed up on the "shore" and no longer good for an "ocean voyage."

I Tim. 2:8 "I will therefore (have) the men to pray in every place, lifting up holy hands..." To "pray" is to have male oral sex, and lifting up "secret" hands is the erection of the phallus by several men.

I Tim. 2:9 "In like manner, also the (young holy) women in seemingly guise with (feigned) modesty and discreetness, to adorn themselves... (but) to what is becoming to professional women in fear of God, by good works." This was their profession, to *appear* to be virgins or pretend to be modest and make themselves attractive, these were prostitutes who lived in fear of God (Arrius Piso), and whose purpose was to do "good works," That is, to give pleasurable fornication.

I Tim. 2:11 "(by) good works (pleasurable fornication) let a (holy "Church") woman learn (her profession) in quietness (and) in all subjection (to men); but a woman to teach (others) I do not allow, nor to exercise authority over men, but to lie (there) in quietness...(as a sacred whore)."

I Tim. 3:1 "If any (phallus) stretches forward to overseership (over shadow) of a good work (sexually pleasurable fornication) he is (must be) desirous (desired)."

I Tim. 3:4 "(of) his own house, ruling well, children having in (his) subjection with all gravity (authority)..." Meaning a man can do whatever he wants to sexually with his own children, and as we have read earlier, they are supposed to obey and do whatever he wishes. Because this is what "Jesus" wants them to do.

I Tim. 3:12 "let those who serve (apparently "in the Church") be husbands of one wife (so they will tire of her and desire a whore) ruling well over children and their own houses (their own little castles)."

I Tim. 3:15 "... God the living pillar..." Didn't we mention what a "pillar" was before? Now, this drives the point home. A "living pillar," a "living phallus," or the prime male sex member.

I Tim. 4:5 "for it is sanctified by God's word (logos = phallus) and by (sexual) intercourse."

I Tim. 4:10 "It is, for this, we both labor..." This is saying "we both labor" in the act of sweaty sex.

I Tim. 4:12 "let no one despise thy youth; but a pattern be of the believers in (the) word (phallus), in (sexual) conduct, in love (fornication), in (the) spirit (horniness), in faith (focus on sex during the act), in purity (in single mindedness on sex and/or clean body for sex).

I Tim. 4:14 "... with laying on of the hands (male sex organs) of the elderhood." The dirty old men of the Church get to lay their "hands" on the young ones as well.

I Tim. 5:1 "An (Church) elder do not rebuke sharply, but exhort (him) as (if) a father (and to) younger (males) as (their) brethren (male sex partners)..."

I Tim. 5:17 "The (Church) elders who take the lead well (are) of double honor, let (them) be counted worthy, (most) especially those laboring in (the) word (phallus) and teaching (sex to) children..."

I Tim. 5:22-23 "Lay hands on no one quickly, nor share in (sins) of others." That is simply to say to stick to the things that turn YOU on. "Keep thyself pure (single-mindedly thinking of sex and clean of body). No longer drink water, but use a little wine on account of (the lack of it in) thy stomach and frequent infirmities." This is advice about impotence. "Wine," we have found, is a euphemism for semen.

And this is because "water" was changed into "wine" by making the connection between the two – in literature. And we already knew that "water" was a euphemism for semen. Oh, and while we are on the subject, the "blood" of Jesus is also secretly "semen."

I Tim. 6:4 "... he is puffed up (erect), (but) knowing nothing..." In other words, he has an erection, but no one to fornicate with. This echoes of the saying, "all dressed up and nowhere to go."

I Tim. 6:11 "... faith, love, endurance..." That is, "focus or concentration upon the sex act during the course of it," and "love," you already know means "fornication." Endurance, means a long-lasting erection and prolonged sexual intercourse as a result.

THE BOOK OF II TIMOTHY

II Tim. 1:4 "... that with joy (sexual pleasure) I may be filled (with semen)..."

II Tim. 1:13 "... in faith and love which (is done) in the (worship of) Christ (phallic God) Jesus (Arrius Piso)." Faith and love. Remember what those mean? Concentration or focus upon the sex act during intercourse, and fornication.

II Tim. 1:14 "The good deposit committed (by thee) keep by (the) Holy Spirit which resides within us." The "pleasurable deposit," i.e. semen. The "holy spirit" is the "secret horniness."

II Tim. 2:1 "Thou therefore, my child, (you must) be strong (to endure the fornication) in the grace (whatsoever is given you) in Christ Jesus." (i.e. "this is your lot, accept it.")

II Tim. 2:6 "The husband-man ("brother," male sex partner) much labor before partaking of the fruits (of his labor)." We've covered this already. "Labor" is hard, sweaty sex, and the "fruits" of that "labor" is the semen of his orgasm.

II Tim. 2:8 "Remember Jesus Christ raised (his phallus) from among (the) dead (state)..." Yeah, that was a really some "miracle" wasn't it?

II Tim. 2:11 "Faithful (is the word; for if we died together with (faith), also shall we together (live again)..." Faithful, is concentrating upon what gets you off while you are in the act of having sex. The "word" is "phallus," and "died" means losing an erection. And "live again" is to have an erection again.

II Tim. 2:22 "But flee (from) youthful lusts, and pursue righteousness, faith, love, peace, with (all) those that call on the Lord out of a pure heart." At first glance you would think that the author is talking about "teenaged lusts" – but NO, he is referring to the desire of toddlers for toys! They considered that a waste.

To them, what was "right" was having sex; all kinds of sex, all the time! "Pure heart" is purely horny desire. We've already covered "faith," "love" and "peace."

II Tim. 3:6 "For of these are those who (are) entering into houses and leading (away) captured silly women laden with sins, which were) led away by (their captores) with various lusts..." The Romans burst into houses of common people abducting young boys and girls to use as Church prostitutes – and the soldiers who performed this duty were the first to have their way with them; raping them.

II Tim. 3:17 "... to every good work fully fitted." That is, "pleasurable fornication," fully fitted (tightly around the prime male sex organ).

II Tim. 4:6 "For I already am being poured out, and the time of my release is come." Now, is the sexual message here missed by anyone? His semen is "pouring out" and his sexual release has come.

II Tim. 4:7 "... I have finished, the faith I have kept." He kept focused upon his fornication and by his relentless "faith," and by the phallic God, he "finished" (by coming to a sexual climax).

THE BOOK OF TITUS

Titus 1:4 "... peace (sexual gratification) from the God Father and (the) Christ (phallus) Jesus (Arrius Piso)..."

Titus 2:2 "... sound in faith, in love, in endurance..." Already explained.

Titus 2:4 "... lovers of children..." Yes, here it is again.

Titus 2:7 "... holding forth a pattern of good works..." "good works" is "pleasurable fornication."

Titus 2:9 "Bondsmen to their own masters (are) to be subject in everything well-pleasing, not contradicting (them)..." Repeating the same command to slaves that was stated previously.

Titus 2:14 "... zealous of good works..." Having "zeal" in pleasurable fornication.

Titus 3:1 "... to be ready to (do) every good work..." Being "ready" to do every pleasurable fornication, means to be erect.

Titus 3:3 "... serving various lusts and pleasures..." Says it all right there.

Titus 3:5-6 "... renewing of (the) Holy Spirit (secret horniness) which he poured on to us richly through Jesus Christ..."

Titus 3:8 "Faithful (is) the word..." Keep concentration on the phallus. But this is also a way of saying that Arrius Piso wrote as Philo as the word "faithful" is spelled "Pistos" which is synonymous with "Piso" and reading the phrase it says, "Pistos (Piso) is the Word (God/Logos)." Meaning that he is the Christian God, and he is the Logos of Philo, because he wrote as Philo.

THE BOOK OF PHILEMON

Phile. 1:3 "... peace (sexual gratification) from God (phallus) our Father (phallus) and Lord (curious/phallus) Jesus (phallus) Christ (phallus)."

Phile. 1:5 "... thy love (fornication) and faith (concentration upon the sex act during sex)..."

Phile. 1:7 "... by occasion of they love (fornication), because the bowels of the saints have been refreshed by thee, brother." The "bowels" of those who were to become future saints were "reamed out," cleaned or "refreshed,"... by a male sex partner.

Phile. 1:9 "... for the sake of love (fornication)..." "... and now also prisoner of Christ Jesus." They were joking about how they had burst into the homes of common people and taken away children to become prostitutes in the Church brothels.

Phile. 1:12 "but thou him (that is, my bowels), receive..." This is saying to receive the entry-way to his bowels, i.e. "anus" for sex.

Phile. 1:16 "... a brother beloved... (is a "brother" indeed!)." This is a "brother" (male sex partner) being "loved" (fornicated). When the central theme is KNOWN all they need do is *infer* the rest of a sentence.

Phile. 1:17 "If therefore me thou holdest a (sexual) partner (then) receive him as me..." That is, "fornicate with someone else also."

Phile. 1:22 "But withal also prepare me a lodging..." Sexual innuendo abounds within the New Testament, in the form of allusion and euphemisms particularly. A "lodging" is a place to "go into." So, this may be seen in a sexual way in addition to the superficial meaning.

THE BOOK OF HEBREWS

Heb. 1:1 "In (so) many (sexual) parts and in (so) many ways (to have sex)..."

Heb. 1:5 "... thou art my son, for today I have begotten thee (acquired), (once) and (then) again (we have known); I will be like to him (this boy) as a father and he shall be (obedient) to me as a son." The speaker is not talking about a baby, as he is talking to the boy so the boy is old enough to understand him, and he has apparently had sex with the boy and is planning to keep him as a sex slave.

Heb. 1:10 "... and works of thy hands..." That is, "the fornication (masturbation) of the male sex organs."

Heb. 1:13 "... sit on my right hand until I place thine enemies (as) a footstool for thy feet." Remember that we had discussed the words "foot" and "feet" as euphemisms for the male sex organ/s? A footstool is something that you put your "feet" upon. This statement is saying that an enemy will be down on their knees and that the conquering person will have their prime male sex organ upon that person as a footstool. In other words, the conquered person will be subjected to the humiliation of being used sexually for anal sex. This, in case you as a reader are not familiar, is an ancient practice which was done by the conqueror to the conquered. This practice goes far back into antiquity. The phrase "right hand" equals "erect phallus."

Heb. 2:7-8 "... the works (fornication) of thy hands (male sex organ)... all (fleshy) things did thou (make) subject under his feet." This means that Arrius Piso, as the great conqueror and the most powerful person in the Roman Empire even above the Emperors in certain instances, has his choice of anyone at all with which to have sex if he so chooses.... "all fleshy things (sex organs) are subject under his "feet" male sex organs."

Heb. 2:13 "And again, behold, (it is) I and the children (in the state) in which the (phallic) God gave (authority to) me."

Heb. 4:12 "for living (is) the word (phallus) of God (Arrius Piso)..."

Heb. 4:13 "... but all (fleshy) things being naked and (then) laid bare to the eyes (multiple anuses)..."

Heb. 6:2 "... and faith (concentration on the sex act) in (the worship of the phallic) God, of the doctrine of washing and of laying on of hands (male sex organs), and of the resurrection (re-erection) of the dead (un-erect fleshy things)..."

Heb. 6:10 "... and the labor of love..." Yes, a "labor of love." We know WHY it was a labor of love, they were "laboring" hard in fornication!

Heb. 8:11 "And not at all shall they (have to) teach each (one) his neighbor (woman) and each his brother (male sex partner)." No, they should already know how to do various sex acts as they were practicing out in the open for all to see during each of the monthly Roman sex fests – and at other times as well.

Heb. 10:13 "... his enemies (into) a footstool for his feet." We have just covered this above.

Heb. 10:22 "... in full assurance of faith..." Yes, and we know what "faith" really was to them. It was the focusing upon or concentrating upon the sex act while it is occurring. There is faith. Have concentration upon what you are doing while you are doing it that "faith" can see you through to the end (climax)!

Heb. 11:38 "... in (upon) mountains and in caves, and in the holes of the earth." Okay, a mountain was synonymous with a phallus, but it was also an allusion to Arrius Piso as "Montanus."

Since they obviously considered the female prime sex orifice to be much larger or gapping as compared to the anus, which they seemed to prefer, one may deduce that "caves" is a reference to the female prime sex orifice, whereas "holes" in the earth, appears more likely to be a reference to the anus.

Heb. 13:1 "let brotherly love abide..." Ah, yes... "brotherly love." That is, "male sex partner, fornicating."

THE BOOK OF JAMES

James 1:3 "knowing (so) that the proving (proof) of your faith works out (of) endurance." "Knowing" is fornicating. So read; "fornicating so that the proof of your concentration on the sex act fornicates out (to the climax/orgasm) because of your endurance (or persistence)."

James 1:14-15 "But each one is tempted by his own lust (whatever turns a person on) being drawn away and being allured... then lust having conceived, gives birth to sin... but sin having been conceived gives birth to sin... but sin having been completed brings forth death (that is to say, the un-erection of the prime male sex member)." Yes, all of this is correct... once you understand just what is really being said.

James 2:15-16 "Now if a brother or sister be naked and destitute maybe of daily food, and anyone from amongst you say to them, "go in peace" "... be warmed and filled..." This is about incest, but not necessarily so. The male "brother" gives to the "sister" his "food" (semen), while she gives to him "suck" from her breasts, and she and he are "warmed" by sex and she is "filled" with his semen. When you get used to reading these texts as they were written you will see that the authors were very deliberate in just how they wrote these texts as they were writing on several levels; not just one, as the general public have been used to thinking.

James 2:17 "So also (is) faith, (for) if it have no works, (it) is dead by itself." You know what "faith" really is now, and "no works" means no fornication. And so this is saying that simply thinking about sex is not going to produce the desired result. The "works" (fornication) is 'dead' because it never started.

James 2:18 "show me thy faith apart from thy works, and I show thee from my works my faith." This echoes "you show me yours, and I'll show you mine." This is saying concentration upon the sex act apart from the act itself is of no value (as indicated above this passage), but that by his "works" (fornication) he is showing proof that he had "faith" (he concentrated upon the sex act while he was having sex).

James 2:20 "But wilt thou know, O empty man, that faith apart from works is idle (dead)?" By now you should be able to see how they just figured out different ways to say the same things and make those appear to be "words of wisdom." What is said here is "will you fornicate? Oh, empty man (meaning that he is empty because he has already "reached" his climax, that concentration on the sex act apart from fornication is nothing more than idle thought. They wanted people to ACT upon their urges, to become horny and go to the brothels.

James 2:22 "Thou seest that faith (concentration) was working (in) his works (fornication), and by (his) works (fornication) (his) faith (concentration) was perfected (made better)."

James 2:24 "You see then that by (his) works is a man justified (in his faith), and not by faith only (alone)." The purpose or justification of "faith" (concentration upon the sex act) is the completion of the sex act. As if they have not already said this enough times in several different ways. But they wanted to make it *appear* that they were really saying something else. That is why they wrote it as they did. The intent was deception.

James 2:26 "For as the body apart from spirit (horniness) is dead (not erect). So also faith apart from works is idle (dead)." This is saying that thinking about sex without actually DOING IT is "idle." Or does not count.

James 3:5 "Thus also the tongue (is but) a little (sex) member; and boast great (fleshy) things. Lo, (such) a little fire, (but) how large a wood (log) it kindles..." Are there any of you who have read up to this point that are still not convinced of the true sexual nature of the New Testament texts? Don't worry, you will be!

James 3:6 "... thus the tongue is set within our (bodily) members..." And so, they have made certain that we now understand how important the tongue is when it comes to sex.

James 3:12 "brethren, my fig tree is able (!)..." Oh, yes, this had already been discussed (elsewhere) that a "fig tree" was also a euphemism for the male sex organs. This is so because a tree is hard and stands erect. But the fig tree also has soft, "fleshy" fruit that is similar to the male testes. And so together, the hard (erect) tree, with the fruit like the male testes, is representative of the male sex organs. So, now read that passage knowing this.

James 4:1 "(Is it) not thence, from your pleasures; which (caused the) war in your (privy) members" In other words, "there's a war going on below, in your sexual area and you need "peace." And we already know what "peace" means (peace = sexual gratification).

THE BOOK OF I PETER

I Peter 1:2 "... of God the Father (of the "God-Father"), by sanctification of Spirit (horniness), unto obedience and sprinkling of blood (semen) of Jesus (Arrius Piso) Christ (phallus): grace (whatsoever is given) to you and peace (sexual gratification) be multiplied." I.e., "have lots of sex (in the brothels)."

I Peter 1:13 "Wherefore, having girded up the loins of your mind..." Oh, what humor! "Girded up the loins of your mind!" What this is actually saying is that you have wrapped around sexual ideas securely away from your foremind (forethought or conscious mind) so that sex is not on your mind – as they would like people to have sex on their mind all the time and just live to visit the brothels.

I Peter 1:21 "believe in (the phallic) God, who raised up (erected) him up from among the dead (un-erect prime male members)."

I Peter 1:22 "... through Spirit (horniness) to brotherly love (male sex partners fornicating); unfeigned, out of a pure heart (sexual essence) one another love (fornicate) ye fervently (feverishly)."

I Peter 2:5 "... as living stones..." The "living stones" are the testes of the male. This is already well-known by many scholars.

I Peter 2:17 "show honor and love (fornication) to all the brotherhood; fear (the phallic) God, (and) honor the King (of Kings)." The "King of Kings," even though this is the title that "Jesus" carries, in the Roman Empire means the Roman Emperor. He is the King over all of the kings throughout the Roman Empire.

I Peter 2:18 "Servants (slaves), being subject with all fear to masters, not only to the good and gentle, but also to the (sexually) wicked." This is advising slaves to give in to the sexual demands of their masters.

I Peter 2:22 "... neither was guile (wickedness) found in his mouth..." Oh, that nasty old "guile"... now how is this sexual? That "wickedness" in his mouth is that sinful semen that was deposited there.

I Peter 3:8 "... loving (fornicating with) the brethren (male sex partners)..."

I Peter 3:18 "... having been put to death (not erect) in (the) flesh (fleshy things), but made alive (erect) in the Spirit (horniness)..."

I Peter 4:3 "... having walked (fornicated)..."

I Peter 4:5 "... who is ready to judge (the) living (erect) and the dead (non-erect phallus)?" Well, certainly with having many sex slaves that they compared the male sex members of each of them, judging them by size and shape.

I Peter 4:6 "... as regards men in (the) flesh (fleshy things, sex members); but might live (become erect) as regards (the living phallus) God in Spirit (horniness)."

I Peter 4:8 "but before all (fleshy) things among yourselves having fervent love (fornication)..."

I Peter 5:4 "... a crown of glory that (will) not fade away..." The word "crown" as we had already discussed is a reference to the head of the prime male sex member. Yes, when the phallus is erect and the "crown" of it is seen at the top, it IS a glorious thing. It will not fade away because people will continue to have erections.

I Peter 5:9 "... firm in faith, knowing..." Yes, very firm and erect, in that "faith" (concentration on the sex act), while "knowing" (fornicating).

I Peter 5:14 "Salute one another with a kiss of love." "Salute" means the raising of the "hand," and that is another way of alluding to a rising phallus. So, a rising phallus, and a wet, sloppy "kiss" of fornication.

THE BOOK OF II PETER

II Peter 1:7 "... and in brotherly love, love..." That is, "male sex partners fornicate, yea! fornicate!"

II Peter 1:18 "... on the holy mount..." Again, "holy" means "sacred" and sacred in turn, means "secret." So, "holy" by this connection, means "secret" as well. And "mount" is a euphemism for something that is rock hard that stands tall. In other words, an erect phallus. And "mount" too, as has been discussed, also is a reference to Arrius Piso as "Montanus."

II Peter 1:19 "and "morning star" shall rise..." This is an allusion to "Jesus" having been invented as Arrius Piso's "spear" or weapon. This will be explained in greater detail elsewhere, but with regards to this being a sexual statement, "evening star" was the name of Achilles' spear in Homer's 'The Illiad.' And so, we know that "spear" was also used as a euphemism for a phallus, and we see here the phrase "shall rise."

II Peter 2:10 "... and especially those who (are) after flesh (fleshy things, i.e. sex organs) lust after pollution walk." Doesn't really make sense does it? Well, you have to remember that Greek has a different syntax or sentence construction than English. Anyway, this says that people lust after "dirty sex" (w/ prostitutes).

II Peter 2:13-14 "... in their deceits, feasting (the sex fests) with you, having eyes (anuses) full of adulteress (ideas)..." "...having a heart (desire) exercised in craving children of curse (that is, who are accursed because of their lot in life)." In other words, they desired (non-royal, "cursed") children as sex slaves.

II Peter 2:18 "... (a) great swelling (with words)..." "... they allure with (the) desires of flesh (fleshy things, the sex organs)..."

II Peter 2:22 "... and as to the sow, (she) washed in the mud (of her) rolling." The "sow" is the whore or prostitute who washed with the semen that her "rolling" around in the bed had produced from her male sex partners.

II Peter 3:3 "... according to their own (particular) lusts (they are) walking (fornicating)..." In other words, this is saying "whatever turns them on and gets them off," as was said before elsewhere.

II Peter 3:17 "therefore, you (are) beloved (being fornicated), knowing (fornicating) already..."

THE BOOK OF I JOHN

I John 2:12 "little children... your sins are forgiven you (for you know not what you do)." Now how is it that little children have done all of this "sinning" through the abuse of adults, that they even NEED to be forgiven for them???

I John 2:28 "And now, little children, abide (be) in him... (as he "abides" in you)." Oh yes, they surely have abided in little children for hundreds of years.

I John 3:7 "Little children, let no man deceive you... (or you get what you deserve)." This is just another one of those "disclaimers" that they had placed throughout their literary works. Many, if not all, of these writers were lawyers and knew the importance of putting in disclaimers and of making them not appear to be disclaimers.

I John 3:18 "My little children, let us not love (fornicate) in word, (but in deed)." ["but in deed," inferred]

I John 5:21 "Little children, keep yourselves from idols (teraphim, the phallic substitutes). He is telling the children to stay away from fake phalli, because it is better to have the real thing.

THE BOOK OF II JOHN

II John 1:4 "I rejoiced (had sexual pleasure) exceedingly since I had found thy children walking (fornicating)..."

II John 1:5 "... that we should love (fornicate with) one another..."

II John 1:6 "And this is... love (fornication), that we should work (fornicate)..." "... that in it you may walk (fornicate)."

II John 1:12 "... and mouth to mouth, (so) to speak, that our joy (pleasure during sex) may be full."

THE BOOK OF III JOHN

III John 1:2 "Beloved (those being fornicated) concerning all (fleshy) things..."

III John 1:3 "For I rejoiced (had pleasure during sex) exceedingly..." "even as thou in truth walkest (fornicate)."

III John 1:4 "I have no joy (sexual pleasure) greater than these (fleshy) things that I should hear about my children in truth walking (fornicating)."

III John 1:12 "... and thou knowest (you fornicate)..."

III John 1:15 "Peace (sexual gratification) to you... Salute..."

THE BOOK OF JUDE

Jude 1:2 "... peace (sexual gratification), and love (fornication) be multiplied."

Jude 1:7 "... having given themselves (over) to fornication and having gone after other flesh..."

Jude 1:8 "yet in like manner, also, these dreamers defile flesh (fleshy things, sex members)..." The term "dreamers" here appears to refer to those who are not concentrating upon the sex act during sex; they do not have "faith" in what they are doing... and as a result they do not achieve an orgasm.

Jude 1:12 "These are in your love (sex/fornication) feasts, sunken rocks (depleted testes), feasting (in sex) together (as an orgy) fearlessly, grazing (here and there among all of the flesh) themselves..."

Jude 1:20 "But you, beloved (being fornicated), on your most holy faith (secret sex thoughts), building yourselves up (getting erect) in the Holy Spirit (secret horniness) (by) praying (male oral sex)..."

Jude 1:23 "... hating even the garment (which is) spotted (soiled) by the flesh (fleshy things)." Many garments got stained or spotted with semen with all the sex that was going on in Church 'sex rooms.'

THE BOOK OF REVELATION

Rev. 1:4 "and his eyes (were) as a flame of fire." You know what "eyes" meant (anuses).

Rev. 2:18 "who hath his eyes like unto a flame of fire?" Well, with all of the anal sex in which Arrius Piso and Pliny the Younger were having... One can only imagine. But it appears that Arrius Piso after all, may be the champion of anal sex between the two.

Rev. 2:22 "I will cast her onto a bed... (and have my way with her)" Another example of inferred meaning.

Rev. 3:18 "anoint thine eyes with eye salve." Well, we already know what "eyes" mean... but the author of 'Revelation' was actively trying to give us the answers to many, many things regarding key words with alternate meanings (euphemisms) and other things having to do with the invention of Christianity.

Rev. 4:6 "four beasts, full of eyes before and behind..." Now, this really tells us a lot. But since we already knew that "eyes" is a euphemism for "anuses," this serves as confirmation. Yes, by stating this, the writer is affirming what we had already discovered. This is so because the two words ("eye" and "anus" in Greek are almost identical). People have the eyes in the front that they see with, and they have an "eye" (anus) behind them.

Rev. 4:8 "full of eyes within: and they rest not..." He appears to be saying that Arrius Piso was obsessed with anal sex, never giving his sex slaves any rest.

Rev. 5:6 "having seven "horns" and seven "eyes." He is really saying something here. Every man has one "horn" (male sex organ) and each has one anus; so seven men would have what is described in this statement.

Rev. 7:17 "shall wipe away all tears from their eyes." Well, "tears" is a metaphor for semen in this instance, but is used generically for bodily secretions also. So read, "shall wipe away all ejaculate from their anus."

Rev. 19:12 "His eyes (were) as a flame of fire." Again, he seems to be pointing out the fact that Arrius Piso was addicted to anal sex.

Rev. 21:4 "shall wipe away all tears from their eyes." You know, when we examine these statements as literature there really isn't any need for the full statements unless they were written with the intent of including specific information. With the statement above, "shall wipe away their tears" would have been enough. But the writer NEEDED to include the rest of the statement as that was the basis of the statement itself. He had already made the same statement before, but by repeating it he wanted to make certain that the reader would understand that he was trying to emphasize what was stated in this passage. There was a REASON for him saying what he did as he did.

CHAPTER III

UNDERSTANDING THE ROYAL LANGUAGE

This is such a new concept that it is even very difficult to know just where to start explaining. There will have to be a number of examples given here for the purpose of illustrating the various points made. All of this is inter-related with so many other things that must first be understood.

It has been very difficult to think of just how to explain all of this new information in any truly structured fashion as it is so new and involves several new concepts which have never been considered by traditional scholars before. This is because in order to do so, they would have needed to have been able to view history itself from an entirely different perpective. And another reason is that there is simply too much of it, and too little time. What has been found are things that ordinarily may not have been found or known of in one lifetime. It took many generations for all of this to have been invented and perfected in antiquity. The greatest pains were taken by the inventors to make sure that this all remained hidden and that they, the authors and inventors not be easily discovered.

We will see the use of alias names being used in ancient times, and things that we would term red herrings, double-entendre', outright lies, white lies, and half-truths. To understand the Royal Language, one has to first understand and comprehend the New Classical Scholarship which is what is used to examine the theory called the Royal Supremacy Theory.

When it comes to explaining things that are so entirely new and different, many times it takes several attempts to convey the meaning of each separate concept or idea. And so, that makes it a real challenge to explain these very new and different things each and every time they are written about.

THE ROYAL LANGUAGE: KEY WORDS AND PHRASES

John 16:33, "I have overcome the world (!)" Means, "I have conquered the world!"

John 18:28, "... for I am king." In Greek, "Oti Basileus eimi ego." In the Royal Language, "I am the Ti(tan) King!"

What has been observed is the use of acrostic initials (which, as any scholar knows, were used in the Bible), and also abbreviations. Therefore, we have learned that a combination of these were being used to disguise what was really being said by the authors. Here are a few examples:

The word "persuading" ('peithon') is used in Acts 19:8. It is actually being used to convey the meaning of two words because it is made up (in essence) of the parts of two words. One is the name 'Piso' in Greek as 'Pei(son)' and the other is 'Th(e)o', which is 'God'. So, what this renders is 'Piso God'. The part that is 'Pei' is an abbreviation for 'Peison'. But you would never know it unless you already knew what to look for! And the reason that 'Thon' is 'Theo' ('Theon') is because of a rule in the Royal Language whereby double letters can be used. In this case, the 'h' in the 'Th' is doubled and the 'h' becomes an 'e'. So, it looks like this, 'Thhon' ('Theon'). Another word that is used to say the same thing is "disobeyed" ('hpeithoun') in Acts 19:9. Here we have, "The Pei(son) ['Piso'] Th(e)o ['God'] U(mmidius) N(icomachus)," or "The God Piso Ummidius Nicomachus." Which is using letters as acrostic initials for Arrius Piso's alias names of Ummidius (Quadratus) and of Nicomachus ('The Victor of the Battle').

Sometimes, a letter like 'z' is used to give the 's' sound. An example of this would be the word 'Thriz', which is the word for "a hair" (as found in Acts 27:34). The result is "Th(eo) Piz(o) ['Piso']" or "Piso God." We see the 'Th' as an abbreviation for 'Theo', which is the word for 'God'.

And we see the letter 'r' as a 'p' because the Greek letter for 'r' ('rho') is written to look/be identical with the Latin 'p'. And so, the 'r' is interchangeable with or may be seen as a 'p'. And this is how the Royal Language worked. That is why in other places we will find a 'v' being identical or the same as an 'n', as the Greek 'n' is written the same as the Latin 'v'.

And here is a neat little phrase by the author of the gospel of John (who was Justus Calpurnius Piso, Arrius Piso's son). He says in John 15:15,

"… of my Father…" The word 'of' is 'ap' in Greek, which is the acrostic initials for 'A(rrius) P(iso)'. So, read "A(rrius) P(iso), (is) my father." Clever, isn't it? This is one way that we collect clues as to who the author is of any particular text.

In John 3:2, we read, "… that from God…" Which is "oti apo Theou" in Greek. In the Royal Language it reads, "The Ti(tan) A(rrius) P(iso) O(ptimus) [is] God." We also consider the fact that there is some syntax involved and so the words do switch around to make better sense of what is being said or to clarify the meaning. So, this could also read as, "The Titan Arrius Piso is God Optimus." Saying this would identify him with the Trajan that Pliny was speaking of in his Panegyricus when he said that 'Trajan' received the name 'Optimus'. However, that does not necessarily mean that Arrius Piso WAS the Emperor Trajan. After some considerable thought, the conclusion became that Arrius Piso was a silent co-ruler with Emperor Trajan and used the name 'Trajan' (the same name as the emperor) just as he did when he co-ruled for a short time with the Emperor Titus. This will be explained in detail elsewhere.

Here is something else on this… in Pliny's Epistles (Book II, of II, pg. 289, where he is talking about Christians), he mentions this phrase twice; "the name of Christ." So, saying it twice, he is emphasizing it. What is he alluding to? Here is the result, "Christ" in Greek is 'Xpistos'. Which, in the Royal Language is 'X' ('Ch'), 'ris' ('Pis'), 't', 'o', 's'. That is, "Ch(rist) Pis(o) T(itus) [or 'Titan'] O(ptimus) S(abinus)." Or it could read, "Piso (is) Christ (the) Optimus Titus Sabinus." In John 4:36, the word 'reaps' ('o Therizon') is used to say; "The God Piso Nicomachus" (as 'The The(o) [God] Piso N(icomachus)," which is "The God Piso, Victor of the battle ("of Garaza," or the battle with the Jews)." However, this should be enough to be a bit of a lesson in the Royal Language.

THE ROYAL LANGUAGE: CIRCLES AND STRINGS

What are "circles and strings" in the Royal Language? They are 'circles' and 'strings' of key words.

Circles of key words are key words which come back to the original key word after going in a 'circle'. What is the reason for this? It was a way of verifying or of proving that the words were indeed 'key words' and purposely used because of their meaning and relationship to other key words. It is like connecting them to insure that there could not be any mistake as to their actual meaning.

And what are 'strings'? They are key words which are strung together to 'say' something that would be incomprehensible/invisible to anyone who cannot read the Royal Language. This too, was another way of proving that the words used were indeed used deliberately and thus, were 'key words'.

Strings were used to construct lines or phrases as well as complete sentences. Knowing about these 'circles' and 'strings' of key words in the Royal Language is what will finally prove to people that what we have been saying for so long is actually true - the Roman Piso family wrote the New Testament and invented Christianity!

Here is an example of a 'circle'...

THE CIRCLE OF LIFE

(Flavius) Josephus' Vita (life) = bios (life) = vios (is 'new' [the new 'law', i.e., the 'new' testament] as neos, phonetically as the letters 'V' and 'N' are the same in the Royal Language, but 'V' is also 'U', and so...) = uios (Which is 'son'. That is, 'Jesus' as the 'son' of God). And Josephus' (Arrius Piso) 'Vita' ('bios') can be "Piso" in this way; 'V' changes with 'F' (as 'PH') and 'PH' is the same as 'P', thus, 'Pios' (Pius/Piso). Also, 'Pio' is 'Piso' as either 'Pia' or 'Pisa' can be the feminine form of 'Piso', the male form can be either 'Piso' or 'Pio' (as seen used by a female descendant of Arrius Piso). Piso as 'Jesus' is "the Life," i.e., 'The Vita'. And the circle is complete.

But we have this directly from the horse's mouth!; Pliny saying "the Law laid down" ("laid down the Law," the 'new' Law - Christianity and the New Testament!), 'Jesus is made to say (in John 10:17); "I lay down my Life ('Vita')." When Pliny said 'laid down', he meant "written down." So, here we have 'Jesus' (Arrius Piso) saying that he has "written down his Vita." What 'Vita'? The only one that makes sense, the 'Vita' of Flavius Josephus - because 'Jesus'/Arrius Piso is the same person who "wrote down" the 'Vita' of Flavius Josephus (Arrius Piso!). Pliny's statement is in his Epistles, Book II (of II), the Loeb Classical Library edition, page 267. 'Jesus' says that he is 'the Life' in John 14:6, as he says, "I am the way, the truth, and the Life ('Vita')..." Remember, when they say something more than once, it is done for emphasis. Just so that there isn't any mistaking this, 'Jesus' is "the Light" (of the world), and so, in John 1:4, is said; "the Life was the Light..." (and thus, visa versa; "the Light" (of the world), i.e. 'Jesus' was the "Life" ('Vita'). And there you have an example of a 'circle'. Next, you need to see an example of a 'string'...

THE PIUS TITAN STRING

We find this example in Acts 28:15, "… us as far as (the) market-place of Appius and three…" Which, in Greek is as follows; "hmin achri Appion Phorou kai Trion." Decoded, it reads, "The Min A(rrius) Ch(rist) Pi(so) [is] Appian, Phar(a)o(h) and Pious T(itan)…" The name 'Titus' was synonymous with 'Titon' (phonetically 'titan'), so one could also mean the other - just like letters that were interchangeable in the Royal Language (and also "Pi(so) Ch(rist)…"

Some things, granted, were spelled phonetically in the Royal Language. But again, one must understand just what the purpose was and therefore, understand the reason for them so doing. By the way, Arrius Piso was writing to himself as 'Appian' when writing as Flavius Josephus. Also, as you will remember, we had already discussed the fact that 'the Min' is what the Jews called the Pisos. 'The Min' were the itho-phallic gods of the Egyptians. Which is appropriate for Piso, because as 'Jesus' he is secretly a phallus. This too, is something which had also been discussed before. The truth is that the Christian God is really secretly a phallus. So, remember this the next time you see Christians praying and worshipping their God.

THE WORD 'DENARIUS' BEING USED AS A QUESTION (In The New Testament)

The word 'Denarius' was used by the authors to very cleverly form a question, but not just any ordinary question. It was a question that was in line with the rest of the things that he (Julius Piso, son of Arrius Piso) was trying to indicate in The Revelations! In Greek, 'Den' means "did not," but was used as a very flexible word where "did not" could have meant it as a reply such as "(I) did not (do it)" or it could have also been used as the preamble to a question, as in "Did not… Arius (do it)?" So that 'den' together with 'Arius' as in the word 'denarius' (which is a monetary unit or coin denomination), would form a sentence that was a question.

Seeing the word "denarius" as two words run together, but disguised only as one and forming the question "Did not Arius (do it)?" Means that a) the question should be examined, and b) fully determined to be as it appears to be. As well as c) answered. We can now do that.

A) "Denarius" as two words run together ('Den' and 'Arius'), is "Did not Arius (do it)?" In the same way that we find sentences elsewhere in the New Testament where portions of the sentences are missing or all of the words not used in those sentences, because of that language and the syntax of that language. We know to fill in those sentences with the words that are inferred to complete the sentence. Most times the 'missing' or inferred words are "I", "of", "and", "the". But in this case, "do it" is inferred.

B) We can determine that in fact this was because of all of the other deliberate examples made by this author in this very same work. So, there isn't any doubt that Julius Piso did indeed mean for us to find his use of the word "denarius" as really being a very clever way of saying and indicating something of importance.

If "denarius" were not comprised of two separate words (one of which is a name), that, together formed a question - the literary device would not have worked. But since it DOES, then it must be seen as intentionally used, and not just deliberate - but very, very clever as well. And so, the question has already partly answered itself (again, deliberately), because it is about 'Arius'. Here it is again; "Did not Arius (Arius who? Piso!) do it?" The author knew that IF anyone were able to see this as a question, as he had intended, that they would also have already figured out who was "Arius". And if they knew that, and they knew that the mention of a "denarius" represented a question about "Arius" - then they should also be able to answer that question.

C "Did not Arius do it?" What was it that Arius did? We know that already, don't we? He wrote as Flavius Josephus, and as Philo of Alexandria, and he invented and played Jesus in Gospels that he was also writing and he helped found and build "The Church" - in short, he invented the Christian religion. And THAT, is the answer to the question. Yes! He DID do it! What is interesting about this is that this question was asked in The Revelation, and it was answered in the Talmud by the Jews (even BEFORE we saw and recognized that this question was even there!). The Jews KNEW this, and that affirms that this is indeed actually a deliberate question pointing to the person who was the inventor of Jesus and the founder of Christianity - Arius (Arrius) Calpurnius Piso!

THE EUCHARIST - EATING THE BODY OF CHRIST

Why the Eucharist (or 'Communion')? This is something else that is explained by our work to expose the truth about the making of Christianity and the authorship of the New Testament texts. It is most interesting to discover just how and in what ways the authors of the New Testament were playing games with letters, names, words, phrases and the language itself as they were composing it. And also, just how they tie so many things together in order to achieve certain results or to make certain that a particular joke of theirs would work or be discovered.

Yes, in a way, the Eucharist is a joke. This is so as it is a play upon certain elements involving Arrius Piso... the person who had invented and played Jesus in the New Testament. But as with many of the things that these people did, it was done on a rather sophisticated level - and that too, was done intentionally.

The purpose for this being that if something is done in a more sophisticated way, it will not be as apparent to as many people; and in fact, may not be discovered at all unless a person already possesses the information which would allow them to understand. In other words, a person must be extremely well educated and understand a great deal about the subject itself. In this case, one is required to know that one of Arrius Piso's alias names (identities) is Ti. Claudius Aristion.

How is this so? Well, we have already (elsewhere) discussed Arrius Piso as Ti. Claudius Aristion (you can find that discussed in Abelard Reuchlin's 'The True Authorship of the New Testament' as well). We find the tie-in when we discover that in Matt. 26:26 'Jesus' is made to say, "Take, eat; this is my body." And we then look back at what was said in Matt. 22:4, "... Behold! My dinner, I (have) prepared..." The word for dinner there is 'ariston' (Aristo). So, only when we know that Jesus is really Arrius Piso and that Arrius Piso had used the name Ti. Claudius Aristion, do we make the connection and understand what is really being said.

So why eat 'Jesus'? Why eat his body and drink his blood in remembrance of him? Because he is 'dinner'! That is, because he is (also) 'Aristo'! And this is the real reason for this becoming a part of the Christian religion! That is the real reason, purpose and origin of the 'holy' Communion in the Catholic religion! It is secretly a joke. It was the inventor of that religion making a joke about himself being 'dinner' (Ariston). By the way, 'dinner' can be virtually any main or regular meal, including breakfast. You cannot see this word in an English translation. It is in the Greek texts. The word is used in Luke 11:38, and Luke 14:12 as well.

This too, is the secret joke of the 'Last Supper' as well. As they are sitting around eating and drinking. When this is studied further, we learn that there are many 'running' jokes or jokes that are linked together by the various elements in them. There is another little joke which is tied in to the Eucharist and that is the phrase that is used in the New Testament "eat, drink, and make merry."

That is because the part 'make merry' is really another way of saying 'have sex'. So, you will find that phrase repeated throughout the New Testament except with the last part left off in most places. That is because instead of actually 'saying' it, it is instead only 'inferred'. That way, it is not as noticeable. Which, of course, was one of their main goals while they were composing the New Testament texts. They wanted to say many things, but not in a way that people would be able to 'understand' all of what they were doing.

There are many 'inside' jokes throughout the New Testament texts and most often than not, one thread leads to another. Such is the case when we have found that 'Jesus' (Arrius Piso) is 'dinner' and he says to eat and drink, we follow the words and phrases that correspond to this. Again, we have already discussed elsewhere, the issue of eating, drinking and being (making) 'merry' (see Luke 12:19, etc.).

And we have already discussed the many sexual jokes that are also to be found in the New Testament texts. Like the way that we find things said in the works of Pliny the Younger and in the works of Flavius Josephus, we find many things that were said in the New Testament by way of reading "between the lines". This is done in many cases by many people everyday to clearly understand what is truly meant by the words in documents. (see the work on the words and phrases in the works of Pliny the Younger) The writers of the New Testament were hiding, ever so slightly, the true meaning of what they wrote by making them appear in a different context.

Here are some examples:

Luke 22:15, "... eat this (!)" John 4:32, "... he said unto them, I have meat to eat..." This is said in a sexual nature and recalls what 'Jesus' said to the children when he asked them if they were hungry and they said 'yes'. They loved to keep the sexual jokes rolling on. After all, they were Romans... and that is one of the things they are known for! John 4:33, "... the disciples therefore said to one another, "did anyone bring him (anything) to eat? (34) [And] Jesus says to them, "my meat (!)"

The New Testament is full of statements of this kind. But people never see them, never think that they could even BE there! Most people read a translated and/or interpreted version of the New Testament and think that that is all there is to it. They have no idea what a difference it makes to be able to read and understand what was actually written there - to 'see' it in the original Greek and to know the meaning of the things which were put there by the authors themselves. Oh, and since you now know about this, do a good service for humankind and let others know about it as well. Particularly those who are effected most by it; the believers in that religion themselves!

Regarding the statement that "made merry" means "have sex," I, Roman have done a lot of work in the area of the Royal Language and in the use of key words by ancient royals in their literary works. My intent is to explain this fully in upcoming works as it is, as I like to say, rather 'sophisticated' and involved.

There are 'levels' to their word usage, for instance. The study and understanding of the Royal Language is quite different from that of the common language (or 'superficial' language). In the research, links between various key words have been found, and patterns have been noted emerging, such as 'circles' and 'strings'.

James Ballantyne Hannay did research in this area to the degree that he was able to make various determinations regarding elements of the Royal Language - although, he did not have any idea of just what it was that he was on the verge of discovering. The scholars of Oxford at the opening of the 20th century (pre-1925) undertook the task of creating an encyclopedia that would give the most honest rendering of what actually exists in the Bible.

This encyclopedia is called 'The Encyclopedia Biblica'. Quoting from this encyclopedia, "ate, drank and made merry," the last always a euphemism for sexual and incestuous intercourse, when "all kinds of relationships are loosed" (Encyclopedia Biblica, Col. 1,513).

In repeating what Hannay himself says about the Bible, as it is so very true and the world needs to be aware of this. He says (In 'The Rise, Decline and Fall of the Roman Religion', James Ballantyne Hannay, c. 1925, pg. 217); "The Bible is full of passages too gross for translation, and containing sex words connected with Roman religion." He knew it, the scholars at Oxford knew it. Several others knew about it and were writing books about it. But this was suppressed and hidden.

How do we know that Arrius Piso has the alternate name of 'Titus Claudius Aristion'? It is always complicated to weed through all of the material that is necessary in order to positively deduce any of the alias names in which these ancient authors used. It can be a long and difficult process. But after one has mastered a large part of it, it becomes much easier. And then to explain it to others, that is another challenge!

Okay, let's work backward and follow the elements that are at hand. In the works of Pliny the Younger, we have an index (in the Loeb Classical Library edition). In it, we find (Ti) Claudius Aristion listed. But we also find Titius (form of Titus) Aristo; and so, we see a simple change in the same name. This verifies that he is 'Aristo' (dinner), and therefore, 'Jesus'.

There is plenty of information listed for both of these identities; both matching what we know of Arrius Piso. In the Index of Pliny's works we find that "(Ti) Claudius Aristion, leading citizen of Ephesus." That is in Bithynia, where Arrius Piso and his family had several farms, mansions and villas. He was also president of the Provincial Council of Asia, who was cleared of a charge which was heard at court; Centum Cellae (Pliny VI.31.3).

Listed as Titius Aristo, he is a Jurist who is often cited in the 'Digest' of Roman Law. He was a pupil of Cassius Longinus and a member of Trajan's consilium with Neratius Priscus. Pliny says that he had survived a serious illness (I.22). He supposedly sends letters to Pliny justifying Pliny's light verse (V.3), and Pliny and he discuss legal procedure (VIII. 14). Again, this is found in the Loeb Classical Library edition (in two volumes) of Pliny the Younger's Epistles (letters) and 'The Panegyricus'.

We find still another name in the works of Pliny the Younger which fits Arrius Piso. That name is 'Flavius Archippus' (the Philosopher). We have already deduced another of Arrius Piso's alias names as 'Aristarchus' in the New Testament (Acts 19:29; 20:4; 27:2, and Col. 4:10, Phm. 24), which is a combination of "Aristo" and "Archippus." We also remind the reader that Arrius Piso was given the use of the name 'Flavius' (as Josephus), by Emperor Vespasian.

But he was already a grandson of Vespasian's brother Titus Flavius Sabinus. So it was not only the name 'Flavius' which he was given to use, but also the rest of his (maternal) grandfather's name - which includes 'Titus' and 'Sabinus'.

Also, the 'ippus' ('ippos') part of Archippus is a key word meaning 'horse' (a horse was also called a 'beast', see the notes on this). Ippos was made identical with the name 'Piso' so that they could allude to 'Piso' without being obvious, the same letters in the name 'Piso' as in ippos, but just rearranged. One may also want to note that in Acts 20:4, where Aristarchus is mentioned, so is Pliny (as 'Secundus'). The original 'Dynamic Duet'!

Also, Arrius Piso used (or was addressed/identified with/by) the inherited name of his ancestor Aristobulus (again, we see 'Aristo'), in Romans 16:10. Here, he is called Aristobulus, but this was done also to honor the name of his Herodian ancestor Aristobulus, a son of king Herod

'The Great'. Besides these things, we have Arrius Piso's use of his 'Titus' name in several other places - and this is not to mention our evidence that Arrius Piso had co-ruled with the Emperor Titus for a short time. One must remember that Arrius Piso was considered a 'great man' by those who were in power in Rome at certain times. There is plenty of evidence present in the literature of the time and that includes the New Testament itself.

Using a literary device of the Royal Language, Julius Piso (Arrius Piso's son) writes in Rev. 2:29, "He that has an ear, let him hear what the..." "what the" is composed of the letters 'TI' and 'TO', which, is to say, "Titus." So, we read it thusly, "He that has an ear, let him hear 'Titus' (aka Arrius Piso!)..." He says the very same thing (for emphasis) in Rev. 3:22.

There is much to be read in the New Testament once one is able to read it as the authors had composed it. Sentences that appear to have only one clear meaning begin to appear more clearly when one is able to see just how deliberately they were constructed. Here is another example. Acts 28:15, "... us as far as (the) market-place of Appius and three..." Which, in Greek is as follows; "hmin achri Appion Phorou kai Trion." Decoded, it reads, "The Min A(rrius) Ch(rist) Pi(so) [is] Appian, Pharo(h) and Pious T(itan)..." The name 'Titus' was synonymous with 'Titon' (phonetically 'titan'), so one could also mean the other - just like letters that were interchangeable in the Royal Language (and also "Pi(so) Ch(rist)..." Some things, granted, were spelled phonetically in the Royal Language. But again, one must understand just what the purpose was and therefore, understand the reason for the writers doing so. By the way, Arrius Piso was writing to himself as 'Appian' when writing as Flavius Josephus. And as we have already discussed elsewhere, 'the Min' is what the Jews called the Pisos.

PISO-GOD, JESUS CHRIST!

This information should be substantial to those who understand it - both those who are familiar with the scholarly aspects of researching ancient history and those who are not as familiar. The reason being that this is illustrative of certain ways that things were stated by ancient writers without those things being obvious to those who were without understanding or wisdom.

The ancient writers loved to do things such as this example shows. They would use words that contained names, PISO being an example of that. And they did so by abbreviating the name! So, that those who were looking for the full name/s would not recognize what they were looking at. Those who would be searching for the name PISO for example, would not be looking for "PIS", they would be looking for PISO. But what these researchers do not realize is that it was a very common thing in those times to use abbreviations, and this is demonstrated perfectly on how the Roman Emperor's name was put onto coins.

A coin of the Roman empire might read; "IMPTCAESVESPAUG" for example. That would translate to: "Imperator (Emperor) Titus Caesar Vespasian Augustus". So, now one can see how names would be abbreviated so as to 'hide' them in literature. "Piso" or Pisone would not be PISO, it would be "PIS". And now that you know this, let's talk about how the phrase "Piso-God Jesus Christ" was put into the New Testament.

We find our example in Romans 3:22, where the word for "faith" in Greek is used; "… faith (of) Jesus Christ,…" The word "of", by the way is not there in the ancient texts, but it is inferred. It was put there to cause what is said to make sense to Christian believers. And the word for 'faith' being "pisteos", so that it reads - "PISteos Jesus Christ." It is the exact same thing that is found in Romans 3:26.

"PIS" is "Piso", abbreviated. And "teos" is really "dios", which is "God".* So, the word "faith" secretly disguises "Piso-God", and "Piso-God" was deliberately put in front of (or as a part of) "Jesus Christ" so as to read (for those who could understand it); "PISO-GOD JESUS CHRIST"! So, wherever you see the word "faith" in the New Testament, think of this and remember that in the original Greek it is "Piso-God"!

And this is why it is so important for scholars and researchers to ignore English translated versions of the New Testament and only use those that give the original meanings of each and every word; and to be able to make sure that the meaning of each word is exact. That is why it is always best to use books that give both the English and the Greek showing the words together so that the reader will know without any doubt. For this example, a Greek-English Interlinear New Testament, by Georhe R. Berry was used, and it can be purchased from Zondervan Publishing, located in Grand Rapids, Michigan.

* Teos, can also be 'Theos', or 'Dios' - meaning 'God'.

THE TRUE MEANING OF WORDS IN 'THE REVELATION'

Those of you who know about the Piso Project Research may know that we have found the author of The Revelation to be Julius Calpurnius Piso, who was a son of Arrius Calpurnius Piso. It now appears that Julius Piso had help writing The Revelation from his son who was also named Julius Calpurnius Piso. And this is because Julius C. Piso, the father, was busy as a general in the war between the Romans and the Jews of 131-2 to 135 CE. The authority for writing the ending of the Jesus story or of 'finishing' the New Testament was given to Julius Piso by his father Arrius Piso. For more information about the authors of the New Testament read "The True Authorship of the New Testament", by Abelard Reuchlin. There is so much to learn about the whole of The Revelations in terms of what the true meanings in it are, of what is being stated. But of the things that we do know of, they are demonstrative and are the key to our learning the rest of the meanings.

Rev. 1:1; "The revealing of Jesus Christ..." Which is just what The Revelation is. After persons learn just what the true meanings are of what Julius Piso was writing in The Revelation, they will know that it really is the 'revealing' of Jesus Christ - for who (or what) he really was!

Rev. 1:3; "the time is near..." Yes, that is right. The time is near... and that is because you are reading the revealing of Jesus Christ! You are reading The Revelation, which, is 'revealing' to the reader just who "Jesus Christ" was (Arrius Piso, Julius Piso's father). And, at the same time, Julius is pointing to both the word 'time' and 'near' as key words in the Royal Language.

Rev. 1:8; "I am the Alpha and the Omega, beginning and ending..." This was Julius Piso stating what "Jesus" is supposed to have said. It is also a way of pointing to his father Arrius Piso as also being/playing Jesus. He says this because "Arrius" starts with an 'A' (alpha) and "Piso" ends with an 'o' (omega).

Rev. 1:10; "I heard behind me a loud voice as of a trumpet." Remember that he says "behind me". He does two things here. (1) He jokes about flatulence "behind him" sounding like a "trumpet" and we know that this is the case from our research regarding ancient Roman jokes and the dirty jokes that have been found in other places throughout the New Testament. In saying this, he also establishes the saying about people talking out of their behind. (2) He makes a reference to a device used by early Priests, where a long tube was used to make 'thunderous' and loud voices that were supposed to make worshippers think that a god is speaking to them at the altar. The tubes made the Priests' voices sound loud and authoritative or 'god-like' and even to resound upon the altars, which fooled the worshippers who were sacrificing at the altars. Remember the 'trumpet' and what it means as you will see that Julius makes more use of this meaning later on in 'The Revelation'.

And once again, we remind you that people who study ancient texts are used to thinking in terms of finding only *one* meaning for words. But when people understand the Royal Language, that should change. Because one of the goals of those writers was to give alternate meanings to the things which they wrote. That meant that they intended more than one meaning for the words that they used; and in at least some cases, they were thinking in terms of the more meanings per word, the better! It was, at times, like a game with them to see who could pack the most meanings into the items that they wrote.

Rev. 1:13. Here, he is describing "Jesus" (Arrius) as the "son of man", which means "descendant of Adam" or "the second Adam." This is also said elsewhere in the New Testament, but Julius is making sure that you don't overlook this. He says that he (Jesus) is clothed in a garment to his feet, which means that "he is cloaked in a veil of mystery," and he has a golden breastplate as the ancient Jewish High Priests also wore. So, he is saying that 'Jesus' (or rather the person that Jesus really was, i.e., Arrius Piso) was really a High Priest.

Now, the reason that Arrius Piso was referred to as "the second Adam" was because the person who played "Adam" in Genesis was the same person who invented the Jewish religion. He was the Pharaoh who founded the Twelfth Dynasty at Thebes, Egypt. And Arrius Piso was the person who played his character "Jesus" in the new religion which he was making!

Rev. 1:14; "… and his head and hair (is) white as if white wool, as white as snow." What Julius is saying is that the sideburns and facial hair of "Jesus" (aka his own father Arrius), were white and that his whole head appeared "white" because all of his hair was white. He lived to be quite old. Arrius Piso died in the year 119 CE, having been born in the year 37 CE. So, he was about 82 years old when he died. But this may also have been his way of pointing to Arrius Piso as being called 'Trajan' by Pliny and of Arrius Piso co-ruling with the emperor Trajan, as we have discovered in our research.

And Julius speaks of Arrius' hair as likened to wool, because he is alluding to his father as the wolf in sheep's clothing! By the way, he is supposed to be describing Jesus and yet he says that he is old and white-headed!!! But this could NOT be the Jesus in the story as he died at the age of only 33! And the word for "wool" is "erion," which is "Arrion"/"Arrian" and therefore either "Apion" or "Arrius" in the royal language, and this points to Josephus and Arrius because; (1) Josephus wrote "Against Apion" (which was only Arrius writing to himself as he was both Josephus and Apion/Arrian/Arrius, and (2)"Apion"/"Arrian" is merely another form of "Arrius".

Rev. 1:16; "out of his mouth, a sharp double-edged sword going forth…" In other words, he, Jesus/Arrius speaks "two ways" at the same time. This is Julius Piso's way of telling us that the New Testament was written two ways; one is by use of the common language and the other is by the use of the 'royal language'.

Rev. 3:10; "The whole habitable world." Make note of this phrase as it is used over and over again in the works of Flavius Josephus and is one of many of the 'correlation's' between the works of Josephus and the New Testament. Julius is giving this and many other key phrases in The Revelation. The full and true meaning of this particular phrase must be explained elsewhere, but briefly, it refers to the new religion that they were inventing as being a "universal" or "catholic" religion. The reasons for this will be explained in another book.

Rev. 3:18; Julius brings up the dirty joke about "eye-salve" (see the section in this book dealing with the irreverent elements in the New Testament); "… And anoint thou with eye-salve thine eyes, that thou may see (know)." He is speaking to the readers of 'The Revelation' en masse and so in the plural, hence the expression "thine eyes" instead of "eye" in the singular.

Rev. 4:3; Julius is describing the breastplate of Piso sitting on his throne, indicating that Piso was both a Priest and a king. The breastplate contains twenty-four stones. He goes further to say that a particular council is made up of twenty-four elders, who all wear the white garments and who are all kings (as they all wear gold diadems or crowns). He is really just speaking quite frankly and saying just how things were. The key is in taking the time to analyze what he is really saying and that is only done by knowing what is the true meaning of his words and phrases.

Rev. 5:8; Julius refers to Jesus as "the Lamb," which we already know is "Arnius" as "Arrius" in the royal language. Jesus is the lamb, therefore, the lamb is really Arrius (Piso).

Rev. 5:10; "… and didst make us, (back) to our (Amon Ra) God, kings and priests; and WE shall reign over the earth." Here Julius explains what the situation really is; kings and priests ruled over the entire known world in that time. It is amazing when one thinks of it, just how much he gets away with saying in The Revelation.

Rev. 6:6; Here is where Julius is really showing his true genius as he not only inserts his father's name into The Revelation by using the word "denarius" (den-arius), but he also makes this as a question… a question that also points to Arrius as the person who invented Jesus and Christianity. This has been explained elsewhere above.

Rev. 6:12; Julius writes about how natural occurrences were used to fool the masses by Priests; (1) Earthquakes, and (2) an eclipse of the sun, as well as (3) the red moon. And, Rev. 6:13, (4) He speaks of "falling stars," which were really meteors. More about this will be explained by us in our other books.

Rev. 6:16; "wrath of the Lamb" = "wrath of Jesus". He is saying that "Jesus" was NOT the gentle person that the Gospels make him out to be, but he was actually a very vicious man - his own father!

Rev. 7:14; "The blood of the Lamb" Julius repeats many of the same words and phrases in The Revelation, but this is done for specific reasons - to get you to notice them! He says "the blood of the Lamb" to draw attention to his father writing as Josephus saying that HIS blood was given to save people, so that the correlation between the two may be made, i.e., "Josephus" = "Arrius" = "the Lamb" = "Jesus").

Rev. 8:2; Seven "trumpets" for seven "angels" ("angel" as a euphemism for "leaders of a church," and "trumpets" meaning just what was explained already. And keep this in mind, because the real payoff in realizing this as the true meaning is about to show itself in The Revelation.

Rev. 8:6; "And the seven "angels" having the seven "trumpets," prepared (positioned) themselves (so) that they might sound (their) "trumpets". In other words, Julius has all seven of the church leaders or priests of the seven churches of Asia on their knees with their rumps up in the air ready to flatulate or blow their "trumpets"! You are now reading what The Revelation really says and you are learning plenty about the meanings which were conveyed by the words that were used. In so doing, you can now also see that these were just persons who possessed a greater degree of knowledge than the masses of the day, that these persons were royals and priests.

Rev. 9:9; "and the sound of their "wings" (were) as (the) sound of chariots of many horses running to war." Here, Julius is telling us that "flying" angels does not mean literally flying, but that this is a euphemism for "traveling fast by chariot." So, "angels" (church leaders/priests) "flying" is now exposed to us for what that really means (this will be expounded upon in other books). Nothing at all supernatural, just a play on words… just as is all of the rest of the bible.

Rev. 9:17; "… the heads of the horses [ippos/Pisos] (were) as heads of lions…" This should be easily seen by those who are familiar with what "lion" refers to in ancient history. The lion is a symbol of royalty. So, the meaning is that the heads of the Pisos were as the heads of royals - that is, crowned as kings… because that is what they were.

Rev. 10:4; "And when the seven thunders spoke their voices…" The use of "thunder tubes" at the altars of the seven founding Christian churches is what is meant here. Obviously, they were still using those old "thunder tubes" at the altars to make people think that 'god' was speaking to them.

Rev. 10:7; "…when he is about to sound (the) trumpet, (he) should also finish/end the mystery of God, as he did announce/say/promise in the glad tidings (Gospels) to his bondsmen, the prophets."

"John", or rather Julius who played John in the Gospels, was one of those bondsmen and prophets whom were promised by Arrius Piso that the "mystery" of "God" would end. In other words, it was agreed upon by all parties who invented Christianity that it would indeed END one day and that in order for that to happen they would insert ways in which the "mystery" would be known to everyone someday. Again, that is what is referred to as the "grace" of God. These persons "graciously" (but apparently begrudgingly) did give us ways to find out who the real authors were and all of the rest of the essential information about how Christianity actually began… and this is what Julius refers to as he is one of the family members who was most concerned about persons having the ability to find out the truth about this - at least at some point in time.

Rev. 11:2; "And the holy city (Jerusalem) shall they trample upon forty-two months." Well, this was something that again as shown in previous examples was stated AFTER the fact. But a person does not realize this until they understand just what it is that Julius is talking about. He is talking about the Bar Cochba war! And that war lasted from late 131 CE till late 135 CE, a total of 42 months! The reason that he says this is so that we can date 'The Revelation' to a time just after the war - so that we would know that it was being written about 136-137 CE. He does not only mention this once, but a few times just so that you will not bypass it.

He obviously wants the reader of 'The Revelation' to THINK. He shows us that he wants them to call in ALL knowledge that they have in order to find out what his true meaning is in what he has written. He is trying to 'reveal' things to you, not hide them like the rest of his family was doing.

Rev. 11:3; "And I will give (power/authority) to my two witnesses, and they shall prophesy a thousand, two hundred and sixty days,..." Note that a thousand, two hundred and sixty days is 42 months (42 months is 1260 days)! He will mention this yet again in The Revelation so that the reader will have to accept that somehow this is an important number to remember - it MEANS something.

Rev. 12:3; "a dragon". We know that "dragon" is a reference to Jesus as the word for dragon also means "baby boy" and the only "baby boy" in the story told by the New Testament is the baby Jesus.

Rev. 12:4; "And the dragon stood before the woman who is about to bring forth (give birth), (so) that when she should bring forth, her child (which is also HIS, because this is Arrius Piso's invented child, "Jesus"), he might devour (the child/Jesus)." This is simply a play on concept and an allusion to Cronus, who devoured his own sons. The reason being is that this is a way for Julius to 'say' or indicate something that will eventually be found out - and that is that Arrius Piso was a descendant of the person for whom the character Cronus represented.

But these authors were very intelligent and Julius Piso is not an exception. By bringing up the woman giving birth to a baby and then offering it to be consumed by a male, he is also reflecting an important part of his father's own work as Flavius Josephus - the part about the starving Jews during the war of about the year 70 C.E. and the woman who was forced to resort to cannibalism to survive; killing her own baby, then cooking and eating it They had been doing this very same thing for thousands of years! By the way, as you can see, the "dragon" not only stood for Jesus (the son), but also for the father/inventor of "Jesus".

Rev. 12:6; "a thousand, two hundred and sixty days." Again, he points to the 42 months. He wants to reader to find out that The Revelation was written (finished) after the Bar Cochba war. That is after 135 CE, and there are a few reasons for this. As was said before, there are other places in the New Testament where things are mentioned "after the fact" and which are presented to the reader as if the text was written BEFORE the events, so as to give the illusion that this was a "prophesy" that was fulfilled - when in fact, the events had already happened. He wanted to help point that out. Also, by letting the reader know that The Revelation was written AFTER the events that it was speaking of, the reader would then know that there was nothing to FEAR about what it was speaking of as this has already passed. He was NOT speaking of an "End Time" sometime in the future, but of a war that had already ended.

Rev. 13:4; "Who is like the beast?" and, "who is able to make war with it?" Well, when you know that "the beast" is "Piso", because "beast" here means "horse" and horse is "ippos", which is just "Piso" rearranged, then you know the answer to the question. The answer is those who have 'power' as Piso does - other royals. This was the "war in heaven" that is spoken of. "Heaven" was used as a euphemism for more than one thing, but in this instance it was used as a metaphor for "royalty", because those who were royal lived in a "heaven" or a paradise (on earth). When you know just what really did happen in those times and who the persons were who were principle to all of this, it all starts to fall into place and your understanding just builds from there.

Rev. 13:11; Julius speaks of a beast (horse, ippos, Piso) with two horns like a Lamb, and who spoke as a dragon. Well, he is saying (again), that the beast is Piso, and that Piso is "the Lamb", i.e., "Jesus", and that he is also the dragon - all at the same time. He keeps indicating this over and over in 'The Revelation'.

Rev. 13:18; "Here is wisdom. He who has understanding (of what 'The Revelation' says), let him count the number of the beast: for (the) number (of) it is a man's; and the number (of it is) 666." There is a lot about this that has been written. The most basic thing that you would want to do is; (1) Get a copy of "The True Authorship of the New Testament" by Abelard Reuchlin, because it contains information about the "checking number" that is in The Revelation and other important information regarding this.

And, (2) refer to the article online about the Pythagorean number system. Also, more writing about this and making more information available about the number systems that were used then as well will be coming out in other books we are working on. Again, there is so much to all of this that it will take several books to detail even what can be considered the 'basics'.

Rev. 14:11. This mentions "the beast", and the "mark". And when we search the apocryphal Christian texts and refer to our knowledge of ancient

Egyptian words and meanings we realize that Julius is trying to inform us that the "mark" (of the beast/Piso) is a cross! This, we find as we know that in the Egyptian writing "a mark" is represented by a "T", which in turn is how the early Christian cross was represented. So, Julius is tying this all together for us. It is like a rope around all of this which he makes tighter and tighter. Arrius Piso has a 'mark', and that mark is a cross, and this is because in the story he plays Jesus whom he had invented.

Rev. 14:13. Here, as in many other places the word "spirit" is mentioned. Why Julius does this is to let those persons who know the royal language learn of another word that points to the Pisos. The word 'spirit' is used not because Julius is talking about a real and actual spirit, but because by our knowledge of phonetics we can see the word as "Numa", and Numa is one of the main ancestors from which the Piso family claimed descent. How do you like our 'tour' of The Revelation so far?

Rev. 14:14; "(the) son of man." This is where our knowledge of the various meanings of the word "son" comes in. The word "son" means a variety of things in the ancient languages, but in this case it means "descendant". So, we read "descendant of Adam". Which sounds fairly benign until you realize that all of this was really a very tightly controlled family business - a family business of invented religion! And that "Adam" was (1) an Egyptian Pharaoh who founded the Twelfth Dynasty at Thebes, and who (2) had "Adam" as a part of his name, and who (3) played the created character "Adam" in Genesis, and who (4) wrote Genesis, and who also had a son named "Seth"/"Sesostris," and (5) that this son is mentioned by Flavius Josephus (Arrius Piso) as he is speaking of this particular Pharaoh and calls him "Seth" when he is known by the "Sesostris" name as Pharaoh. Also, "Seth" and "Sesostris" are the same name - but Josephus did what he did for a very deliberate reason... and that was so that we could find it and put this all together!

Rev. 15:2. Here Julius mentions "the beast" again, but this time he speaks of its "image", and this makes a person think. What could he mean by this? And then one remembers something that stuck out in the epistles of "Paul" (really Pliny the Younger writing), and that is where Pliny/Paul gives us a riddle. He gives an enigma or riddle and says as in a mirror, face to face. Well, that is an "image". So, it is quiet clear that Julius was trying to get us to pay attention to that passage and by doing so that this would lead us to find Pliny the Younger as a participant in the invention of Christianity as well. If a person does study the epistles of Paul and work on this 'riddle', they will find that some of the particular words and phrases used match up to those that are used in the epistles of Pliny the Younger! And too much so to be a coincidence. This is something that was discovered by Abelard Reuchlin.

The epistles of Paul were written by Pliny the Younger. Julius could also be saying that Pliny the Younger was really also a Piso, which appears to be possible and even probable. He was, in a sense, a Piso according to what we now know... but that too, will have to be left as a topic in another book.

Rev. 16:2. Again Julius mentions "the mark" of "the beast" (Piso). It could have been that Julius Piso was trying to point out to us that just before the emperor Vitellius died he cut off one of Arrius Piso's ears and "marked" him for life. Arrius Piso is the "beast" remember, because his name 'Piso' was made synonymous with 'ippos' (horse) and a horse was called a 'beast'.

Rev. 16:10. He speaks of "the throne of the beast," which is saying that Arrius Piso was also a "king." He is giving us information by saying these things so that we can build up a 'profile' on Arrius Piso from which to work.

Rev. 16:13; "Out of the mouth of the dragon, and out of the mouth of the beast, and out of the false prophet..." Why out of the mouth of all of these three? Because he is telling us that they are all one and the same - Arrius Piso, his (Julius') father!

Rev. 19:13; "and his name is called, The Word of God." Now why would Arrius Piso/Jesus have this name? The Christian believer will think that this means that Jesus is the mouthpiece of God on earth. But what it really means is that Jesus was ONLY words, that he was "the logos" or creation/invention of someone. And by saying this, Julius points us to that person. Surprise, surprise!, it is not Josephus this time, but Philo of Alexandria. Yes, that is right. Arrius Piso also wrote as Philo of Alexandria. And this too will have to be explained in other books.

Rev. 19:16; "And he has upon his garment (clothing/veil), and upon his THIGH a name (that) is written, King of Kings and Lord of Lords." We'll talk more about 'garments' and such in our other books, but for now we want that you concentrate upon what Julius says about something being written on HIS (Jesus') thigh. This is very, very important, as he is again pointing out something about his own father and this time doing it in a way which refers to him as a general in the war against the Jews (Pharisees). Remember that we had told you about Arrius Piso falling from his horse as a Roman general? And in the fall he hurt his leg and this caused him to become lame. What Julius is telling us here is that he not only hurt his leg, but ended up losing it altogether! His THIGH was not flesh anymore, but most probably "wood" and that being such, it could be written upon quite easily without hurting Arrius Piso. Now this also explains several other things. We now can better understand the running joke about a person being "swift of foot", and seeing that this is said in the singular "foot" instead of the plural "feet". We can now better understand the Jewish references to Arrius Piso as the "Lamed Vov", or "Balaam the Lamed." It is in knowing what all of these various things actually refer to that, enables us to understand what exactly is being said and meant, and that requires a great overall knowledge of all things that relate to the subject.

Rev. 20:8; "the four corners of the earth." Here, Julius is inserting a way of making sure that people using science and logical methodology would one day help uncover the falsehood of the Christian texts as he anticipated that one day the entire world would know that the world was NOT flat. All of the royals of his day knew this, but not the common persons; as the common persons were kept in ignorance by the royals. He knew also that by saying this, it would be known by all persons one day that the apparent "errors" in the bible as a whole would be recognized as having been done deliberately so as to be a sort of "red flag" to persons which would say to them "hold on here, this is supposed to be the unerring word of God and yet here are things that are proven to be WRONG! It is apparent that Julius had hoped that the average person would one day be intelligent enough to figure out these things and, by doing so, they would be able to make use of "The Revelation" as he intended, to finally end Christianity by exposing it for what it really was - an invented religion that was created by the Piso family!

Rev. 20:12; "and books were opened; and another book was opened, which is "the book of life." And the dead were judged out of the things written in the books according to their (own) works." Julius is telling us that the ancient authors would come to be known to us, the public, for who they really were one day and that WE, the general public would judge THEM by how they either helped or hindered us in our quest for the truth. The "book of life" being spoken of by Julius was primarily the New Testament, and secondly the bible as a whole, while thirdly, just generically ALL books that recorded information about the royals, their relatives, and ancestors as they preserved their memories and places in history forever.

And this is also what they meant about they, themselves being able to "live forever". They meant that through their literary works, they would "live forever." Another thing that Julius means here when he says "and books were opened," is that in order to find the true meanings of what he was saying in "The Revelation" that a person must read many books and read them well enough to know what he was referring to by what he was saying in "The Revelation".

Rev. 21:6; "I am the alpha and the omega, the beginning and the end." Julius again quotes "Jesus" as saying he is "A" at the first and "O" at the ending; "A"rrius Pis"O". Jesus is Arrius Piso. He is also saying at the same time that Jesus (Arrius Piso) is the beginning of Christianity and he is the key to *ending* it. And he is! Because it is known by many persons that Jesus was not real, but that he was only an invented character (actually a 'composite' character) that was played in the story by his inventor, Arrius Piso… that will be it, the cat will be out of the bag and everyone will know that it was really one gigantic fraud!

Rev. 21:10. Again, Julius uses the word "spirit" and says "great mountain." Well, this could mean that Arrius Piso as "Montanus" in history was also the incarnate of their ancient ancestor "Numa". In any case, he is drawing attention to "Montanus" by his use of the word "Mountain" and he also uses "great" in front of it. This makes one wonder if he was not alluding to "Montanus" (or Arrius Piso) as also being "Varus", as that name is an alias identity of Arrius Piso as well (see our current work on Arrius Piso as 'Montanus').

And how the word "great" ties in here with "Varus" is because "Varus" derives from the Egyptian word "Veru" for "Great man/men". We also see Arrius Piso as "Varus" as exposing him as the founder of the Annii Verii branch of Roman royals. And, this is so because we know that "Annii" is really another spelling of "Arri(us)", while "Verii" is only another spelling of "Var(us)"; and together we have the alias name of Arrius Piso as "Arrius Varus." He (Piso) was also shown to us in history under the alias name of "Varus". And he is known to us as also being the founder of the latter Roman royal line of the "Annii Anicii."

So, when you know the facts, there is really plenty being not only said in "The Revelation," but also being confirmed by literary evidence. He says; "Seal not the words of the prophesy of THIS book (Revelation); because the time is near." Again, he emphasizes that "the time is near." And he is *not* speaking of an "end time" for humanity, but of an "end time" for Christianity! The end is near for Christianity, because you are reading 'The Revelation'; the "revealing" of the truth about the Jesus character, not what is preached in churches.

Rev. 22:13; "I am the alpha and the omega, the beginning and end, the first and last." He keeps emphasizing this because he wants you to figure this out. He wants you to figure out that Jesus is "A"rrius Pis"O".

Rev. 22:16; "I, Jesus, sent my angel (priest/church leader) to testify to you these things in the churches; I am the root and the offspring (read "descendant") of [king] David, and the bright morning star." This is how this passage should be read. And again, Julius is saying a lot here about his father who was playing Jesus. He says that he is "a" descendant of king David... not "THE" descendant of king David as if there were only one. As he knows that there were indeed many. And Arrius Piso was a descendent of king David, therefore "Jesus", his invented character was also.

Julius is really wise to state that Jesus is "the bright morning star," as this says much. He actually shares this title with John the Baptist, who was also really only a character that was invented to represent Yochanan ben Zakai. Julius is saying that "Jesus" was being used as a weapon, that he was a 'spear' and moreover, that he was a spear belonging to Arrius Piso, because of his already having put us wise to the facts. We know that this is so because Julius is making a comparison here between Jesus (and/or John the Baptist) as "the bright morning star" as the name of a spear (of Arrius Piso's) and "the bright EVENING star," which was the spear of Achilles in The Illiad. So you see that he is drawing from all of these sources to explain all of this in fine detail. But one has to do the research in order to understand what he is actually referring to.

Rev. 22:20; "Yes, I am coming quickly," "Amen," yes come Lord Jesus!" Now, some people have taken this to mean that something bawdy is being implied, and that would indeed ring true because of the fact that the New Testament was written by filthy-minded Roman royals. And this is putting it very lightly, as they enjoyed seeing others suffer and die, even making a hobby of inventing the 'best' methods of torture ever imaginable.

However, as yet nothing has been found as proof that the word "coming" in the ancient texts had the same meaning as another spelling of this word does today. This is mentioned only because some other people have jumped to this conclusion. What this will likely prove to mean is simply that the hour is nearing when persons will recognize what he is saying in "The Revelation" and that in doing so that HE will be "living" again via his literary works and that HE will be judged by us favorably because he was the one person who helped us the most to find the truth with his works.

He uses "Amen" to point to their ancient ancestors generically, the Pharaohs - as they received the name/title "Amon" (as in "Amon Ra") upon their ascension to their thrones. And he says "yes, come Lord Jesus," with an inference so that it should read; "Yes, come Lord (kurios/curious/ mysterious/unknown) Jesus (be known for who you really are!)." It appears that he is pointing to the line in the New Testament about "the God that believers ignorantly worship."

Rev. 22:21; "The grace of our Lord Jesus Christ be with you all. Amen." He emphasizes "the grace" which means the graciousness of Arrius Piso to even let the world know of what they had done and of doing this via hints and clues along with bits of literary evidence.

And this concludes our summary of "The Revelation" by examination of it via the use of the royal language and by understanding the things that were really being referred to in "The Revelation."

THE WORD 'ANGEL' REVEALED AS 'HIGH PRIEST' (In The Revelation)

Now as we know Julius Calpurnius Piso to be the main author of 'The Revelation', (see 'The True Authorship of the New Testament, by Abelard Reuchlin) we see that he reveals to us that "angel" is a euphemism for "priest".

Julius Piso's style in 'The Revelation' is to (1) give the essential or important information, and to (2) do so in a way in which those who have wisdom or a good deal of knowledge and intellect may find what he has cleverly placed in it. He knows that anyone who is really looking for answers will read what he has written over and over, and that they will refer to earlier chapters and verses to find out what later verses really mean.

He also knows that persons who will discover what he has left in his work will have a good familiarity with many other works, and particularly, the works of his own father as 'Flavius Josephus'. You will find a great number of key words and phrases that are used by Julius in 'The Revelation' are also found in the works of Flavius Josephus. As a matter of fact, you will find that while Arrius Piso (Julius Piso's father) was writing as Josephus, that he had already had the name that Julius would use as the author and what the title of the book would be.

Arrius Piso, writing as 'Flavius Josephus', places this phrase in his works in several places "divine revelation" (see Antiquities of the Jews). He is very careful to only say "divine" and "revelation", so that you would have to know the inference of what was being said to recognize what was really being said. The Revelation was claimed to be written by St. John the Divine and the full title of it is; "The DIVINE REVELATION of John" or "(The) REVELATION of John the DIVINE." However, the true author (John/Julius), says in the first line of this book that this is "(The) Revelation of Jesus Christ," i.e., the 'revealing' of Jesus Christ.

In any case, the author of "The Revelation" does a very good job of informing intelligent readers of this book about just what are the real and true meanings of many words and phrases. Actually, one of the most important of these is that the use of the word "angel" actually refers to a "priest" and NOT a harp playing, winged entity of a supernatural nature that comes down from a mythical heaven to help humans on behalf of god. There isn't any god, there isn't a heaven, and there aren't any "angels". There ARE, however, priests.

Julius Piso lays the foundation for us to piece together what he is saying. (1) He lists the seven churches of Asia (Asiatic Turkey) (Rev. 1:11). Next (2), he says that "the seven stars (spears/weapons) are "angels" of the seven churches (of Asia)" (Rev. 1:20). And (3), he proceeds to state where all of the seven churches are, but he also states that each has an 'angel'.* And (4) he gives us a 'key' phrase in Rev. 8:2; "And I saw the seven angels (of the seven churches) which stood before God (Arrius Piso); and to them (the "angels"), were given seven trumpets."

What does this mean? Firstly, "trumpets" refer to the "thunder tubes" that were used by the high priests at the altars to fool those who were there to sacrifice into thinking that they were talking directly to god. This was because the trumpets were used like megaphones to make the voice resound with 'authority' as the voice of a god would sound in the minds and imagination of those who were kept in ignorance of all of these things.

So, Arrius Piso, as 'god', gave each of the heads of each of the seven churches a "thunder tube" to use at their altars in order to fool the uninformed people. This was a 'sacred' device, given only to priests. So, the angels are really priests. Need more evidence? There is plenty.

Imagine what it means to finally be able to show definitively that there isn't any such thing as "angels!" This is what Julius Piso allows us to find out because of his "revealing" what he did. Rev. 8:6; "the seven angels (of the seven churches of Asia), ..."

He does what he can to 'say' many things to us, but he also gets us used to "filling in the blanks" as well. That means that he is deliberately trying to get us to understand what he INFERS as well as what he states outright.

In Rev. 8:6, you KNOW that the seven angels that he is speaking about are the same that he has spoken of just prior, so you know that he MEANS "the seven angels of the seven churches of Asia (Asiatic Turkey)," even though he does not say this in that particular verse. He is showing that he wants the reader who can to complete his sentences and who is able to understand his inferences, to do so.

Rev. 9:9; "and the sound of their "wings" (were) as (the) sound of chariots of many horses running to war." Here Julius is telling us that "flying" angels does NOT mean literally flying, but that this is a euphemism for "traveling fast by chariot." So, "angels" were indeed really priests, not flying messengers of god come down from a heaven supposedly located somewhere in space, and "flying" is now exposed to us for what that really means; and that is just going very fast. Nothing at all supernatural, just a play on words. Just as the rest of the bible is/does.

Rev. 14:10; "… the holy angels." Why would anyone have to say that "angels" are "holy"?** In this case, Julius is showing where you can put the word "priests" here in place of the word "angels". And you too, can do this. Wherever you find the word "angel" used, just read "priest" there instead.

Rev. 14:15, 17; "another angel came out of the Temple." Priests come out of the Temple. Rev. 15:6; "the seven angels (of the seven churches of Asia) came out of the Temple." Again, "priests" come out of Temples. Rev. 20:1; "I saw an angel come down from heaven." This means that the priest "digressed" to a more common level. He came down from his comfortable level of a high state of luxury and of great intellect to a low level where the common person resides. THAT, is what this really means.

Priests also had "duties" which they could chose to do or not do. One of those things could be something like that which is described in the works of Flavius Josephus that an "angel" has come to do. You can read between the lines to find what must have happened. There was obviously a man and his wife who were trying to conceive a son, they apparently went to the Temple and confided in a priest that the man was not able to get his wife pregnant. So, the priest pays the woman a few visits "as an angel" or in disguise while the man is away and "helps" the couple to conceive a son. So, the priest, as an angel, "does" the mans wife, and the husband is grateful(!) to the "angel". (See Whiston translation of Jose., page 119) Also note that this is much the same as that section in the Bible that tells about the birth of Samson (of Samson & Delilah).

Julius Piso, just as the rest of the writers of his time, was able to show his meanings in many instances merely by "inference" simply because he knew that no one was able to write anything other than the royals. And that meant that all that was written was tightly controlled and that whatever was said in any of the writings related to places and things that were in the other writings of the time and, knowing this, there could not be any confusion. They were able to deliberately control and maintain all that was written for public consumption so that what would be left to future generations was "pristine" in meanings and relation to each other.

Below are listed the seven original churches which were located in Asia (Asiatic Turkey). Prior to these churches, the builders of Christianity were likely using regular homes to indoctrinate slaves and other uninformed among the masses.

*Rev. 2:1; "The angel of the church of Ephesus."

Rev. 2:8; "… the church in Smyrna."

Rev. 2:12; "… the church in Pergamos."

Rev. 2:18; "… the church in Thyatira."

Rev. 3:1; "… the church in Sardis."

Rev. 3:7; "… the church in Philadelphia."

Rev. 3:14; "… the church of the Laodiceans."

** The word "holy" is the same as the word "sacred", and the word "sacred" means "secret". So, one reads "SECRET angels". The 'secret' is that they are really Priests!

Notes:

Various examples of the word for "angel" are instructive and can be seen as supporting evidence. 'Angel' as 'mighty' (in authority), points to 'angel' as a euphemism for High Priest (in Hebrew as 'abbir', Psa. 78:25). 'Angel' as an agent or mouthpiece of God, also points to 'angel' as a High Priest (in Hebrew as 'malak', Gen. 16:7. Traditionally, Pharaohs and other kings were considered gods with their brothers being High Priests). "Angel" as an authorized agent or representative of God, in Greek as 'aggelos,' in Mark 1:13.

"…the Holy Angels," a phrase in Mark 8:38. Read this phrase now as "the sacred priests." "Angels" as gods and judges, as 'Elohim' in Hebrew (Psa. 8:5); some High Priests were also kings. Many kings were called gods, and passed judgment upon others. Knowing this, is also quite telling when it comes to finding the word 'Elohim' being used in Genesis as well.

Now read "Angels" as "replicated facilitators" of God (in Hebrew, as 'shinan', Psa. 68:17). In case things happened, such as the death of either the first born as successor to his father as king, the second born son takes his place, etc. If the second son as High Priest dies, there are instances of a king being both High Priest and king, and other combinations have occurred according to particular circumstances. What this appears to be a reference to is what is called the successive lineage of High Priests, which can be seen in genealogical tables.

The actual meaning of Luke 20:36 is that 'angels' are human beings and die the same as everyone else. But it is worded to deliberately give the reader a different impression; "neither can they die anymore, for they (after dying), are equal unto the angels/priests (when THEY have died)." Conclusion: 'angel' is a reference to High Priests, not ordinary priests.

BIBILOGRAPHY (AND RESEARCH MATERIAL)

[Note: You may want to search your local college or public library for some of these first.]

"The True Authorship of the New Testament," Abelard Reuchlin, 1986 (Second Edition).

Cost: $8.00. Copies can be obtained from: The Abelard Reuchlin Foundation, P.O. Box 5652, Kent, WA 98064.

"The Synthesis of Christianity," is another book that we will be working preparing soon. So be on the lookout for it.

"The Rise, Decline & Fall of the Roman Religion," James Ballantyne Hannay, 1925. Regarding the creation of the Christian religion by the Romans. Check for availability online.

"Christ and the Caesars," Bruno Bauer, 1877. Published originally in German, in Berlin. Translated copies are available from: Charleston House Publishing, Alexander Davidonis, Publisher. James Island, P.O. Box 12814, Charleston, SC 29422. This English translation is copyrighted 1998. The cost is $54.00

"The Interlinear Greek-English New Testament," George Ricker Berry. Available from: Zondervan Publishing House, 1415 Lake Drive, S.E., Grand Rapids, MI 49506. Send for their catalog for the current price, etc.

"Science and Creationism," Edited by Ashley Montagu. Oxford University Press, 1984. First published by Oxford University Press, New York.

Probably available through major bookstores such as Border's and Barnes & Noble.

"Deceptions and Myths of the Bible," Lloyd M. Graham. Copyright 1975, published 1979 by Bell Publishing Company, distributed by Crown Publishers, Inc. A reprint of the book published by University Books, Secaucus, N.J. Available through major booksellers.

"Jewish Expressions on Jesus," (An Anthology), Edited by Trude Weiss-Rosmarin, KTAV Publishing House, Inc., New York. 1977. May be out of print. ISBN 0-87068-470-1

"Europe And The Jews: The Pressure of Christendom Over 1900 Years," Malcolm Hay. Published in 1992 by Acadamy Chicago Publishers, 213 West Institute Place, Chicago, Illinois 60610. May be ordered through major booksellers.

"Rome of the Caesars," Thomas W. Africa. Copyright 1965. Published by John Wiley & Sons, Inc., New York. Norman F. Cantor, Editor, Columbia University. Thomas W. Africa, Associate Professor of History, University of Southern California.

"The Complete Works of Flavius Josephus," English translation by William Whiston. Copyright 1981, by Kregel Publications, a division of Kregel, Inc. Kregel Publications, Grand Rapids, Michigan 49501 ISBN 0-8254-2952-8

"Gospel Fictions," Prof. Randel Helms (Dr. Randel McCraw Helms), of Arizona State University - Professor and biblical scholar.

"Who Wrote the Gospels?" by Prof. Randel Helms.

"The Mania of Religion," W.F.Dean, 1995, New York; and "Honest to God," 1988.

"Young's Analytical Concordance of the Bible"

Check the Loeb Classical Library either online or offline for:

"Pliny (the Younger), Letters and Panegyricus," in two volumes (in Latin and English), "Apostolic Fathers," in two volumes (includes the apocryphal book 'Barnabas'), "Philo," (in Greek and English), "Seneca," (in Latin and English), "Tacitus," Histories (in Latin and

English), "Tacitus," Annals (in Latin and English), "Historia Augusta," (supposedly by various authors), "Fronto," (in Latin and English), "Frontinus," (in Latin and English), "Plutarch," Lives (in Greek and English), "Flavius Josephus," complete works (in Greek and English), "Appian," circa 130 C.E., "Arrian," circa 130 C.E., "Suetonius," circa 130-140 C.E., "Juvenal," circa 90 C.E., "Martial," circa 100 C.E., "Persius," (the Poet) circa 65 C.E., "Petronius (Arbitor)," circa 65 C.E., "Lucan," circa 65 C.E., "Vellius Paterculus," Roman historian, "Livy," (T. Livius), Roman author, "Virgil," 'The Aeneid', "Ovid," 'The Metamorphoses', "Homer," 'The Illiad', "Plato," 'Dialogues', "Marcus Aurelius," 'Meditations', circa 180 C.E.

SOME REFERENCE MATERIAL FOR NAMES, PERSONS & SUBJECT MATTER

(1) 'Emperors & Biography' (Studies of Historia Augusta) [a book], a chapter titled 'The Bogus Names', by Ronald Syme, 1971. Excerpts from this are as follows; "When the attempt is made to expose a fraud, attack on all fronts is to be commended. Since, however, the grand assault on the HA started from the bogus names, it will be appropriate to revert to that approach, but with a different emphasis, not seeking in the first instance to establish a date for the compilation. "Syme offers a listing of ten considerations for observation of names (nomen), this, particular to the HA, but also applicable to other times and works of Roman history; 1. Indistinctive Names, 2. Imperial Gentilicia, 3. Names from earlier Vitae, 4. Recurrent and favourite Names, 5. The names of the Authors, 6. Names of Classical Authors, 7. Names from Literature, 8. Names of fun and Fantasy, 9. Perverted Names ("One example is clear, using Suetonius, the author changed 'Mummia' to 'Memmia'. That is a mere trifle in the devices of the HA. If an author is anxious to be plausible, he may try to convey an impression of novelty (and hence of authenticity) by names that look original because different.... One trick is to modify the shape of familiar names. Several instances have been detected"). 10. Fictitious Characters, who, by their names (and/or attributes), reflect families eminent in the Roman aristocracy.

(2) 'Tacitus: Some Sources of his Information', JRS, 1982, page 68. (A ref. For Tacitus being' Neratius Priscus'), Ronald Syme.

(3) 'The Composition of the Historia Augusta: Recent Theories', JRS, 1972-73, Ronald Syme (on general considerations in observation and usage).

(4) 'Aelius Aristides', JRS, 1972-73, C.P. Jones (reference for Julius Piso and Pedanius Fuscus).

(5) 'Sura and Senecio', JRS (after 1967), C.P. Jones (reference for Q. Sosius Senecio, i.e., Pliny the Younger, as well as for Julius Frontinus, and Quadratus Bassus).

(6) 'The Consulate of the Elder Trajan', JRS (Journal of Roman Studies), vol.43-45, 1953-55, page 79-80, by John Morris (A ref. for Arrius Antoninus).

(7) 'Calpurnius Siculus and the Claudian Civil War', JRS, 1982, T.P. Wiseman (reference for the Calpurnii Pisos and their claim of descent from Numa).

(8) 'Amicitia and the Profession of Poetry', JRS, 1978, Peter White (on Statius the Poet, and the Pisonian conspiracy).

(9) 'The Bisection of the Books in Primative Septuagint Mss.', The Journal of Theological Studies, vol. 9, 1907-8, H. St. J. Thackeray (on differences in the versions of the Septuagint), also see 'Studies in the Septuagint' (the origins, recensions, and interpretations), by Sidney Jelicoe.

(10) 'New Insight into the Bar Kokhba War and a Reappraisal of Dio Cassius', Jewish Quarterly Review, July 1986, by Mordechai Gichon, Tel Aviv University (Archaeological evidence and reconstruction of events and chronology of the war).

(11) 'Piso Frugi and Crassus Frugi', JRS, 1960, Ronald Syme (on the family of Licinianus Frugi Piso and ancestors).

(12) 'Antonius Saturninus', JRS, 1978-80, Ronald Syme (some on Trajan, Domitius Corbulo, Flavius Silva, and 'Antonius Primus' [Arrius Piso] being Flavius Silva, i.e., 'Bassus' (Also see Suetonius' reference to 'Antonius Primus' as the killer of emperor Vitellius [at the end of 'Vitellius'], and his 'nickname' of 'Becco'/Bassus).

(13) 'Some Flavian Connections', JRS, 1961, Gavin Townend (ref. for 'Paetus', Barea Soranus, T. Flavius Sabinus II, etc., with genealogical chart).

(14) 'The Roman Siege-Works of Masada, Israel', JRS (after 1960), I.A. Richmond (Lucilius Bassus, Flavius Silva, etc., with map of Masada).

(15) 'Some Pisones in Tacitus', PIR (after 1955), Ronald Syme (ref. for Piso family relations).

(16) 'People in Pliny (the Younger)', JRS, 1968-69, Ronald Syme (ref. for nomen and nomenclature, 'Neratius Priscus'/Tacitus, general pedigree of the Antonine emperors).

(17) 'The Friend of Tacitus', JRS (after 1954), Ronald Syme (ref. for Justus Piso and various names/persons).

(18) 'Domitius Corbulo', JRS (after 1969), Ronald Syme (ref. for Pliny and Trajan's ancestry, and conspiracy of the Pisos).

(19) 'The Lower Danube under Trajan', JRS, 1959-60, Ronald Syme (ref. for Justus Piso and his closeness to Tacitus, misc. dates/chronology and other family members and names).

(20) 'Emperors and Biography', Sir Ronald Syme (some genealogical data relating to the Roman emperors).

(21) 'Oligarchy at Rome: A Paradigm for Political Science', Sir Ronald Syme (this work points to the fact that despite the outward appearance of the existence of 'dynasties', there was actually an oligarchy in place which was the real power behind the Roman Empire).

ADDITIONAL SOURCES & REFERENCE MATERIAL

'The Last Age of the Roman Republic', 'The Cambridge Ancient History', Vol. 9, J.A. Crook, Andrew Linott, Elizabeth Rawston, Cambridge Univ. Press, 1994.

'The Oxford Classical Dictionary', Simon Hornblower, Antony Spawforth, Oxford Univ. Press, 1996.

'L. Calpurnius Piso Caesoninus in Samothrace and Herculaneum', H. Bloch, The American Journal of Archaeology, pg. 485-493, 1940.

'Intellectual Life in the Late Roman Republic', Beryl Rawson, Duckworth, London, 1985.

'The Family in Ancient Rome: New Perspectives', Beryl Rawson, Croom Helm, London, 1986.

'Philodemus in Italy: the Books from Herculaneum', Univ. of Michigan Press, 1995.

'The Life And Times of Calpurnius Piso', Ed Champlin, Museum Helviticum, XLVI, pg. 101-124, 1989.

'Piso and Veranius in Catullus', Ronald Syme, Classica and Mediaevalia, danoise d'Histoire pour les etudes anciennes et medievales, XVII, pg. 129-134, 1956.

'Das Senatus consultum de Cn. Pisone Patre', Werner Eck, Antonio Caballos, Fernando Fernandez, pub. Verlag C.H. Beck, Munich, Germany, 1996.

'Cnaeus Calpurnius Piso, Legate of Syria', D.C.A. Shotter, Historia 23, pg. 229-245, 1974.

'Galba', by E. Fabbricotti, Rome, Italy, 1967.

'Some Pisones in Tacitus', Ronald Syme, Journal of Roman Studies, 46, pg. 17-21, 1956.

'The Roman Revolution', Ronald Syme, 1939.

'Oligarchy at Rome: A Paradigm for Political Science', Ronald Syme (Also 'Emperors and Biography').

'The Sons of Piso the Pontifex', Ronald Syme, The American Journal of Philology, 101, pg. 333-341, 1980.

'The Origin of the Veranii', Ronald Syme, Classical Quarterly, LI, pg. 123-125, 1957.

'Piso Frugi and Crassus Frugi', Ronald Syme, Journal of Roman Studies, L, pg. 12-20, 1960.

'Cn. Calpurnius Piso cons.', Werner Eck, Ord. 7. V. Chr, und die lex portorii provinciae Asiae, Epigraphica Anatolica, pg. 139-146, 1990.

'The Historian L. Calpurnius Piso Frugi and the Roman Annalistic Tradition', Gary Forsythe, Univerity Press of America, New York, 1994.

'The Parents of Quintus Piso', R.J. Evans, Phoenix, Vol. 43, pg. 69-70, 1989.

'L. Calpurnius Caesoninus and Transalpine Gaul', S.L. Dyson, Latomus, XXXV, pg. 356-362, 1976.

'Nero: the Man and the Legend', John Bishop, pub. Robert Hale Limited, London, 1964.

'Nero', B.H. Warmington, pub. Norton and Company, New York, NY, 1969.

'Senatorial Opposition to Claudius and Nero', D. Allindon, The American Journal of Philology, 77, pg. 113-132, 1956.

'Ancestor Masks and Aristocratic Power in Roman Culture', Harriet Flower, Clarendon Press, N.Y. 1996.

'Jewish Expressions on Jesus: An Anthology', Trude Weiss-Rosmarin, KTAV Publishing House, Inc., N.Y. 1977.

'The Bible as Literature - The New Testament', Prof. Buckner B. Trawick, Barnes & Noble, 1968.

'The Interlinear Greek-English New Testament', George Ricker Berry, Zondervan Publishing House, Grand Rapids, Michigan.

'The Complete Works of Flavius Josephus', translated by William Whiston, 1981, Kregel Publications, Grand Rapids, Michigan, 49501.

'The Inquiry of Seneca's Treason', W.H. Alexander, Classical Philology, XLVII, pg. 1-6, 1952.

'The Roman Nobility', R. Seager, Oxford, 1975.

'Political Dissidence Under Nero: The Price of Dissimulation', Vasily Rudich, Routledge, London and New York, 1993.

'Pompey and the Pisones', Erich S. Gruen, California Studies in Classical Antiquity, 1, pg. 155-170, 1968.

'Tiberius, Piso and Germanicus', T.T. Rapke, Acta Classica, XXV, pg. 61-69, 1982.

'Nero's freigelassener Epaphroditus und die aufdeckung der Pisonishen vershwoerung', Werner Eck, Historia, XXV, pg. 381-384, 1976.

'Roman Parties in the Reign of Tiberius', F. Marsh, The American Historical Review, XXXI, pg. 23, 1926.

'Literature and Politics in the Age of Nero', J.P. Sullivan, Cornell Univ. Press, London, 1985.

'The Reign of Tiberius', F.B. Marsh, Oxford University Press, London, 1931.

'A History of the Roman World from 30 B.C. to A.D. 138', Edward T. Salmon, London, 1991.

FASTI CONSULARES   (68 To 96 C E)

EMPEROR & REIGN	CONSULARES
68 CE	Nero Titus Catius Asconius
	Silius Italicus
(Death of Nero)	P. Galerius Trathalus
69 CE Galba	T. Vinius (Rufinius?)
(Death of Galba)	
69 CE Otho	L. Savius Otho Titianus II
	(Otho's brother)
	L. Verginius Rufus
	L. Pompeius Vopiscus
	T. Flavius Sabinus (III?)
	Cn. Arulenus Caelius Sabinus
	P. Marius Celsus
	Fabius Valens
	A. Caecina Alienus

Roscius Regulus

C. Quinctius Atticus

(Death of Otho)   Cn. Caecilius Simplex

69 CE Vitelius   No Consulares Listed

(Death of Vitelius)

70 CE Vespasian   C. Licinius Muscianus

                          Q. Petillius Cerialis Caesius Rufus

71 CE   Cn. Pedius Cascus Caesus

                                    C. Calpurnius Rantus

                              Quirinalis Valerius Festus

                                    C. Atilius Barbarus

                                    L. Acilius Strabo

                                    L. Annius Bassus

                                    C. Laecanius Bassus

                                    C. Caecina Paetus

72 CE   L. Lucinius Musianus

                                    T. Flavius Sabinus (III?)

73 CE   L. Valerius Catullus Messalinius

L. Aelius Oculatus

Q. Gavius Atricus

M. Arrecinus Clemens

74 CE   T. Plautius Silvanius Aelianus

Q. Retillius Cerialis Caesius Rufus

T. Clodius Eprius Marcellus

M. Hirrius Fronto Neratius Pansa

75 CE   C. Pomponius ?

L. Manlius Patrunius

76 CE   L. Cassidienus ?

Galeo Tettienus Pertronianius

M. Fulvius Gillo

77 CE   Cn, Julius Agricola

L. Pompeius Vopiscus

C, Arruntius Catellius Celer

M. Arruntius Aquila

78 CE   D.Iunius Nvius Priscus (Rufus?)

L. Ceionius Commodus

Sextus Vitulasius Nepos

Q. Articuleius Paetus

Q. Corellius Rufus

L. Funisulaus Vettonianus

79 CE   P. Calvisius Ruso Iulius

(Vespasian Died) T. Rubrius Aelius Nepos

80 CE Titus   Sextus Marcius Priscus

Cn. Pinarus Aemiluis Cicatricula

L. Aeluis Lamia Plautius Aelianus

Q. Aurelius Pactumeius Fronto

C. Marius Marcellus Cluvius Rufus

T. Vinicius Iulianus

81 CE   L. Asinius Pollio Verruncosus

(Titus Died)

Domitian   M. Roscius Caelius

C. Julius Juvenalis

L. Vettius Paullus

T. Iunius Montanus

M. Petronius Umbrinus

82 CE	T. Flavius Sabinus (III?)
83 CE	Q. Petillus Rufus
	L. Tettius Iulianus
	Trentius Strabo Eruichi Homulus
84 CE	C. Oppius Sabinus
	L. Iulius Urus
	(C. Tullius Capito Pomponianus Plotius Fimus)
	C. Cornelius Gallicanus
85 CE	Q. Gavius Atticus
	L. Valerius Catullus Messalinus
	M. Annius Herrenius Pollio
	D. Aburuis Bassus
	C. Salvius Liberalis Nonius Bassus
86 CE	Ser. Cornelius Dollabella Petronianus
	C. Secius Campanus
	Q. Vibius Secundus
	Sextus Octavius Fronto
	Ti. Iulius Candidus Marius Celsus
	A. Lappius Maximus (Pliny)
	C. Octavius Tidius Tossianus

L. Iavolenus Priscus

87 CE L. Volusius Saturninus

C. Bellicius Natalis Tebanianus

C, Ducenius Proculus

C. Clinius Proculus

88 CE L. Menicius Rufus

D. Plotius Grypus

Q. Ninnius Hasta

M. Otacilius Catulus

Sextus Iulius Sparsus

89 CE T. Aurelius Fulvus

M. Asinius Atratinus

P. Sallustius Blaesus

M. Peducacus Saenianus

A. Vicirius Proculus

90 CE L. Cornilius Pusio

L. Antistus Rusticus

Q. Accaeus Rufus

C. Caristanius Fronto

P. Baebius Italicus

C. Aquillius Proculus

L. Albius Pullaienus Pollio

Cn. Pinarius Semilius Cicatricula

(Pompeius)

M. Tullius Cerialis

Cn.Pompenius Catullinus

91 CE   M. Ancilius Galbrio

D. Minicius Faustus

P. Valerius Marinus

Q. Valerius Vegetus

P. Metilius Sabinus Nepos

92 CE   Q. Volusius Saturninus

L. Venuleius Montanus Apronianus

L. Stertinius Avitus

Ti. Iulius Celsus Polemaenus

C. Iuluis Silanus

Q. Iunius Arulenus Rusticus

93 CE   Sextus Pompeius Collega

Q. Peducaeus Priscinus

C. Cornelius Rarus Sextius Na(so?)

94 CE	L. Nonius Calpurnius Torquatus
	(Asperenas)
	T. Sextius Magius Lateranus
	M. Lollius Paullinus D. Valerius
	(Asiaticus Saturninus)
	C. Antius A. Iulius Quadratus
	L. Sillius Decianus
	T. Pomponius Bassus
95 CE	L. Neratius Marcellus
	P. Ducenius Verus
	Q. Pomponius Rufus
	L. Baebius Tullus
96 CE	C. Manlius Valens
	C. Antistius Vetus
	Q. Fabius Poattuminus
	T. Prifernius (Paetus)
	Ti. Catius Caesius Fronto
	M. Calpurnius …(icus)
(Death of Domitian)	